EveryDay Matters

EveryDay Matters

One Woman Savors Ordinary Days
in Extraordinary Ways

Marie Clapper

Pack-O-Fun, Inc., Des Plaines, Illinois

Library of Congress Catalog Card Number: 96-68414

ISBN 0-9652041-0-3

Published by Pack-O-Fun, Inc., 2400 Devon Avenue, Suite 375, Des Plaines, Illinois 60018-4618. (800) 272-3871.

Cover Concept: Billie Ciancio
Cover Design: Temkin & Temkin, Northbrook, Illinois
Cover Photo of Marie: Robin Pulley, Boston, Massachusetts

To my father — who taught me to enjoy words,
to stop and smell the roses . . .
and dandelions,
and to live in the here and now.

To my mother — who lived the message:
"This is the day the Lord has made.
Let us rejoice and be glad in it."

Acknowledgements

Twenty years ago, Lyle Clapper, against his better judgment, allowed Kay Daugherty Sweeney to hire me – a newly divorced mom trying to get back in the work force – to write for Clapper's <u>Pack-O-Fun</u> magazine.

Fifteen years ago, Lyle suggested I write "One Last Thought," a monthly column, in Clapper's *Crafts 'n Things* magazine.

Last year, my assistant Sue Hetman prodded me along and organized those columns for a possible future book.

This year, the Clapper team of Janet Wilcox, Toni Ballentine, Lisa Behzad, and Sue Hetman diligently and thoroughly transformed that idea into a reality.

During those twenty years, I was helped and encouraged along the way by —

my colleagues here at Clapper who pitched in whenever extra help was needed (especially Debbie Roman, Scott Hoffman, Jim Lui, and Arthur Steitz) and told me repeatedly that this book was the right thing to do;

friends who networked with me, enlightened me, and inspired me, including Lora Wintz, Nolan Bennett, Janet Cheatham Bell, the late Joe Rizzo, Susan and Bob Gleason, Ann Herrera, Howard Greene, Don Frye, Greg Zeis and his pals at PGI, Wayne Beder and Rose Lauro, Dave Rosenthal, Dave Gehrman, Karen Ancona, Ellen Blatt, Mike Hartnett, Bill Gardner, Jim Scatena, Joe Kinsey, Ken Zutz, Mary Ann Blackburn, Gail Starr, Tom and Bonnie O'Connor, Carol Lupino, Joan Green, Jackie Edwards, Patricia Nimocks, Virginia Bauer, Kathy Lamancusa, Mary Strouse, Jerry Zaidman, Bev and Todd Parkhurst, Arlene Rubin, Judy Rubin Rotman, Betty Gardinier, Loretta Harris, Lynnea Semasko, Barrett Rochman, Chrisy Miller, Sue Shuckart, and many others;

readers of *Crafts 'n Things* who thanked me for various "One Last Thought" columns, repeatedly asking me to compile those stories into a book;

and

my children, family, and friends who lived these stories with me and have allowed me to tell them to you.

I publicly and deeply thank these kind and generous people.

And I thank God for guiding me all my life and showering me with blessings — which I have tried to share with you on the pages of *EveryDay Matters*.

Preface

The night the last of our six children, Annie, was born, I looked at her in total amazement as if this were the first child I'd ever held or borne. Out loud I said, "Oh, please, please let me raise her until she has become herself."

You see, I was almost forty-three then and fully aware that I would be sixty-four when Annie turned twenty-one. I might not be around to see her grow up.

If that happened, how would she know me? How would she benefit from the lessons of my years? Who would show her that life overflows with opportunities to laugh, to enjoy, to delight? On her own, would she realize that every day is a wonderment to be savored?

And that is when *EveryDay Matters* began — as a collection of true stories from my life which I wanted to be certain my infant daughter could someday know.

For years, I had written down these stories — my adventures and misadventures, my insights and fears, my failures and personal victories —and published them as monthly magazine columns. With Annie's birth, I began compiling them into the book you now hold.

EveryDay Matters is a reflection of my beliefs: That every day does matter. That to experience joy in life, we must be aware of each day. We must recognize the extraordinary in the ordinary moments, savor them, and remember them — for they are the framework of our lives.

Welcome to *EveryDay Matters*.

Contents

Just Us Girls 83

*Marie tells her favorite adventures with her mother, her
daughters, and her girlfriends*

The Other Half 109

Marie shares true stories about the men in her life

A Life in the Daze of a Woman 147

Marie shows how she has found joy in even the most
ordinary of moments

Still Searching After All These Years

Easy Crier

There are two kinds of people in the world: the easy criers and the non-criers. It's not a matter of choice; everyone is born into one group or the other. Either you have the crying chromosome or you don't.

I do. I inherited the crying gene from my maternal side. My mother — and her father before her — cried freely, openly, and often. As for me, hardly a day goes by when I don't cry — or at least get so choked up I can't speak.

I cry when I'm happy and I cry when I'm sad. I cry when I'm frustrated and when I'm inspired. I cry when I am told a lie and when I discover a new truth. I cry alone, with one close friend, or in a crowd. Old makes me cry. Young makes me cry. A look can move me to tears. So can a tone of a voice — gentle gets an immediate tear, harsh takes a little longer.

Easy criers and non-criers transit the world differently. Non-criers *sing* when "The Star-Spangled Banner" is played at a ball game. Easy criers? By the time I get to "the rockets red glare," I can feel the tears welling up. My first boyfriend was totally confounded by this behavior.

"How can you cry at the ball game? Before anyone even makes an error! What's to be sad about?"

"I'm not sad," I'd try to explain, "I'm moved. I think about America and freedom and the thrill of victory and the agony of defeat and Lou Gehrig and . . ."

"You think about all that before the first pitch is thrown? How can you concentrate on the game?" A legitimate question, I'll admit. I had no explanation. Still don't.

Non-criers sit through entire performances of *Les Miserables* without turning their eyes into swollen, red slits that throb with every beat of the bass violin. By the time the curtain fell on *this* easy crier's first viewing of that show, I had to be shoveled into a bag and carried to the car. The second time I saw Les Mis I was worse! Like Pavolv's dog, I cried *in anticipation* of each heart-wrenching moment!

Non-criers leave social events with their dignity intact. Not I. At more than one wedding, I've cried so much I've been identified as the jilted ex-girlfriend of the groom. At school functions, I am a constant embarrassment to my kids. ("Mom, you were the only one at the Bowling Awards who cried! The only one!") Funerals? Don't ask.

Having been like this all my life, I can tell you honestly, most of us criers are sincere in our tears. We aren't trying to manipulate. We aren't in desperate need of attention. We're no deeper, no shallower, no smarter or dumber than the next guy. We just cry a lot.

I think God did us all a favor when He added easy criers to the mix. Clearly, the mission of the non-criers is to keep the world solid, allowing everyone to move through life with firm footing. But it's the job of any easy crier to keep that solid surface from becoming too hard a crust. And some of us are very, *very* good at our job!

February 1995

Different strokes. Don (the groom) cries when he's happy. So do I (the bridesmaid). Carol (the bride – all you see here is her smile) giggles!

Two Ladies – Pretending

The day before the scheduled sitting for our first formal photo together, Annie was inspired: "Let's dress up like movie stars for our picture, Mommy!" And, as you can see, we did ... or at least tried. Annie and I had a great time getting ready in the studio dressing room — lots of giggling and primping. I wish I'd had a camera myself to capture the photographer's reaction when he got his first glimpse of us in our full regalia!

Long after this photo itself has faded, I'll still remember the day vividly — being a little girl again, making-believe with Annie in Never-Never Land.

The Ultimate Scare

For me, Halloween will be a little late this year: I turn 50 in November.

While all six of my kids keep me feeling young, it's seven-year-old Annie who really puts a spring in my step. Still, there are times when an oldster like me feels dreadfully antique raising a youngster like her.

Like the Open House at Annie's school this fall. Looking at the other parents, I realized I am the oldest mother in second grade. In fact, I am old enough to be the mother of most of the mothers! There may be some over-the-hill fathers in Annie's class, but I'm quite certain there are no other second-grade mothers who learned to jitterbug while watching Justine and Bob on "American Bandstand" in black and white.

Seven-year-olds with older moms know their mothers look different from their friends' mothers. Annie once spent an entire grocery trip trying to convince me to buy spandex slacks. As I pushed the shopping cart around, she showed me with her hands what I looked like from the rear.

"See, Mom, your behind is about this wide and this high and sticks out about this much." She indicated something approximately the size of a large microwave oven. "But if you wore the kind of pants Jennifer's mother wears, your behind would probably look only this high and this wide and stick out only about this much." (For the record, Jennifer's mother is about eighteen years old and wears a size minus 2.) The rest of the day I walked out of rooms backwards.

I can tell Annie thinks I'm really, really old. Recently we had to race from the car to a concert because we were late. After half a block, Annie stopped dead in her tracks and looked at me with her eyes wide open in awe. "Mother! You can run!" she said, mouth agape, as if I were the oldest person on the planet and she were witnessing a miracle.

Having an older mom presents some nifty opportunities though. For example, Annie knows all the words to "Sha-Boom, Sha-Boom" and several other memorable tunes from the 50's. She has at her fingertips authentic costumes from four decades which she can use for dress-up any time. And 50-year-old elbows are covered with turkey skin — a phenomenon Annie finds absolutely fascinating.

The scariest part of turning 50 and having a young child is the thought that I may not always be there for her. I want to mash the potatoes when she prepares her first Thanksgiving dinner. I want to tell her, "You go take a nap, honey. I'll watch the baby." I want to pick her up at the airport and listen to her bubble over about an important business trip. I don't want to miss a single chance at getting to know her.

And I want her to know me, too. I guess one of the reasons I began writing was so Annie would have some way of feeling close to me, no matter what the future.

Just last week, Annie and I sat side by side on the couch making silly phrases that rhymed. We laughed, thought of a few more, and laughed again. "You know, Mom, you're not just my mother," she said with the kind of whistling lisp people with missing teeth make, "you're my friend." She snuggled up to me and added, "I like being with you." Then, unaware, she started tenderly kneading the turkey skin on my right elbow . . . and I knew there was nothing to fear.

October 1992

Fine Dining

My family knows it's almost summer when I order my restaurant meals with the precision of a brain surgeon performing a lobotomy. Intense and dedicated, I operate to remove a gram of fat here, a calorie or two there, from every blue plate special that heads my way — just so I can lose that last five pounds.

I once performed my calorie cutting at a popular fish restaurant in our town. "For my entree, I'd like the filet of sole please," I began, "but I'd like that broiled dry without any butter, margarine, or oil *whatsoever*." (I am convinced that the word *whatsoever* knocks off 37 calories.) The waitress wrote this on her pad.

"I'd like a steamed vegetable, perfectly plain," I clarified. "And I'll have a baked potato — but please be sure there is no sour cream with it, not even on the plate," I urged. The waitress jotted down every instruction.

"I'll skip the soup, but give me tomato juice with a wedge of lemon, please," I requested. She continued scribbling dutifully. "And I want a house salad with house dressing," I concluded, closing my menu, "but put the dressing on the side."

Never breaking stride — still writing feverishly and without looking up — the waitress deadpanned: "Left side or right side?"

Fast food places give me a chance to creatively custom-tailor my food, too. One Saturday afternoon, my daughter Annie and I stopped for lunch at Wally's Hot Dog Stand. I had just thought of an ingenious way to cut 73 calories off my Wally-Dog and was eager to test it.

"I'll have a hot dog with double lettuce, double tomato, and double cucumbers, please," I said to the man behind the Order Here window. "But could you cut the hot dog in half vertically — not horizontally, but you know, up and down, so the half runs across the entire bun?" I asked with a smile. He shot me a dirty look and sighed.

"Put one of the halves on the bun," I said in my perkiest voice, "and can you guess what I want you to do with the other half?"

He stared at me wide-eyed for about twenty seconds. Then, without taking his eyes off me, he shouted over his shoulder, "Wally! I think you better get over here right away! I got a customer harassing me here!" (Truly, all I wanted him to do with other half was put it on Annie's hot dog so she would get more protein.)

One recent evening after I'd placed an especially detailed food order in one of our favorite restaurants, my husband Lyle asked me, "Wouldn't it be easier on everyone, Marie, if you just walked into their kitchen, scrubbed up, and prepared your own food?

"All that fine-tuning is silly! You told the waitress, 'Give me tomatoes instead of potatoes.' Now you're eating mine!" Lyle said as I reached over to help him with some of his French fries. "If *you* eat *food* off *my* plate, *I* get the calories?"

Just then the waitress brought Lyle his dessert, apple crumb pie with ice cream. Lyle took the first bite. I picked up my fork. "Somehow or other, " I said, sounding like Lucy 'splaining to Ricky, "food tastes better when it comes from your plate."

Lyle pondered and chewed. After a minute or two, he nodded and gently moved the pie to the center of the table. "I'm happy to share this with you, Marie," he said, "which means either we've been married so long I finally understand you . . . or this apple crisp isn't as good as it looks." We laughed as we ate the pie together — every last crumb.

Just as I had suspected, it was delicious.

June 1994

Still in the Driver's Seat

As I was driving to the market yesterday, I noticed a pretty girl in a drivers' ed car. Young. Eager. Elated with her new experience.

I started thinking about our Scott who started driving two years ago. Soon Susan and Elaine will be learning to drive, and before I know it Ed and Jeff will be behind the wheel.

Not knowing exactly why, I found myself playing, "What's Wrong with This Picture?" Suddenly I realized what was wrong: I wasn't in the picture!

I don't know how it happened, but somehow, when I wasn't looking, everything shifted. Instead of *my* being the new driver,

Lyle (at his graduation in 1964) holding Scott, Lyle's first child. And in the blink of an eye . . .

the college freshman, the first-time camper, I find myself waving bye-bye as my kids embark on these adventures!

But after all, it's spring. A new beginning. A new life. A new experience. And change is one of the most exciting aspects of life!

No, I'm not "the pretty girl learning to drive" this spring. But you can bet I'll be doing something new, something rewarding, something exciting. And if I'm lucky, that's what I'll do every spring of my life!

March 1982

. . . Lyle's first child Scott (at his graduation in 1987) holding his sister Annie, Lyle's last child.

Current Frustration

Contrary to what my children may believe, electricity has always been part of my life. Just the same, I sometimes wish I'd been born in the Dark Ages so I wouldn't have to deal with it and all its frustrations.

My electrical dis-ease came to light (you should pardon the expression) shortly after Lyle and I married and bought our first home. It was a big, old house and within the first month we blew a fuse. Lyle, my hero, marched to the basement. I, his brave and dedicated new bride, followed.

Lyle held a flashlight on the fuse box as he opened it, and I picked up an old baseball bat lying in the corner and stood by silently. Lyle glanced at me as he began his search for the faulty fuse. A few seconds later he looked at me again. Finally, he pointed the flashlight in my face and asked, "Why are you standing there with that bat in your hand, Marie?"

"I know first aid for electric shock, honey. You shouldn't touch the victim, but you must break his connection with the electrical source using a non-conductor," I said, feeling like a real helpmate.

"So in other words if I get a little shock, you're going to break my arm with that bat to save me," Lyle sputtered. "I'll survive the electric shock but spend six weeks in the hospital with my arm in traction!" At that moment I wished I could tell Thomas Edison exactly what I thought of his invention!

Electronic media like TVs and VCRs are the most frustrating. There was one brief moment in time when I could actually run a VCR without help from my children. Technological enhancements make that no longer possible. Now I require as many as three of my offspring to help me through the experience. I pay dearly for that, believe me. I once heard Jeff tell his friend "what my mom actually tried to do with the VCR." They laughed so uncontrollably that Coca-Cola® squirted out their noses and they both got the hiccups.

Years ago, I had no problem changing TV channels. I would just get up and flip a dial. Easy. Then the improvements began. The remote control. The cable box. In our family room I now am required to use three — count them three — clickers to go from one mediocre program to another. Not only are there three separate procedures, they must be in a certain sequence. I must press the correct buttons on the correct clicker in the correct order or I watch reruns of "The Price Is Right" until dawn!

That three-clicker system is actually progress. Last year (Lyle swears he was trying to simplify things for me) all I had to do to turn on the TV was press one button on the set itself. However, there was a catch: The TV worked for just four minutes. If I wanted to continue watching, I had to turn it on again.

Any idea how often you stub your toe while jumping up to avoid missing an explanation from Columbo? Or what a Cajun recipe tastes like when you omit 30 seconds of ingredients? Or what it feels like to risk it all on Final Jeopardy and never know if you won? I can tell you precisely. And all because I'm not at ease with electricity.

There's still a big part of me that longs for intimate talks in front of a non-electrically sparked, roaring fire. I yearn for romantic dinners by candlelight with background music from a wind-up Victrola. I find the sounds of the cuckoo clock soothing beyond explanation.

Okay, I confess I write all this to you on my up-to-the-nano-second computer with its electronic spell-check, forty-thousand megabyte capacity, and high-powered printer . . .

a handwritten word or two is still the best way to close a note to a friend.

April 1993

A Walk on the Wild Side

I fell in love with Jazzabelle the first time she jumped in my lap and licked some leftover ice cream off my chin. This pretty little Shetland sheep dog has just one problem: She barks and chases cars . . . a lot.

Written indelibly on every chromosome in Jazz's body is the same herding instinct her Sheltie ancestors have always followed. Unfortunately, she doesn't distinguish between sheep and Chevys. She figures, if it looks like it's getting away, bring it back! Bark, jump, do whatever you have to do, but get it back.

Obedience school didn't have much impact, so I collected suggestions from well-meaning friends on how to end that infernal barking and chasing. One Sunday last spring, I was just desperate enough to give those ideas a try . . . all at the same time. I had no idea what an unforgettable adventure it would be.

The plan? To give Jazz "enough rope," Lyle would attach her to three leashes hooked together end to end. Then he'd walk her to the huge parking lot at the high school. Five minutes later, I would drive over with the kids. When Jazz chased our car, Jeff would squirt her with lemon juice, and Annie would shake a jar filled with marbles at her.

The plan started falling apart right after Lyle and Jazz left. I didn't have a plastic lemon, and there was no time to buy one. "Get your super-shooter squirt gun, Jeff, and load it with Sprite," I said, trying sound calm. Jeff stared at me for a full minute. Then he shook his head slowly, as he poured a can of lemon-flavored soda into his squirt gun.

I couldn't find the marbles either. "Annie," I said, constructing my plan as I spoke, "when I give you the signal, bang your shoe against the side of the car. You can make that sound like marbles in a jar, can't you, Sweetie?" I could tell even little Annie had zero confidence in me as a dog trainer.

I had one remaining concern. If Jazzabelle recognized us, all our efforts would be in vain. "Kids," I chose my words carefully, "to make sure this really works, I think we should wear these." I showed them three Lone Ranger masks I had dug out of the Halloween drawer.

Twenty minutes and several bribes later we drove into the parking lot looking like bandits on the way to a heist. Lyle was sitting on a concrete block staring at his watch.

Jazz began to bark and chase our car almost immediately. But when she saw our masks and heard the shoe banging, she must have figured, "Great! A new, fun game!" I swear she smiled, then jumped straight up in the air, and ran in the other direction — barking her head off. I had no recourse but to chase her — and Lyle.

Jazz ran circles around Lyle. The circles got smaller and the leash got shorter until Lyle was wrapped like a mummy in twenty-five feet of doggie leash, his arms trapped at his sides and his legs unbendable. "Marie!" he screamed. "Stop the car immediately." I could barely hear him over Annie's loud shoe-pounding and the barking. "This isn't working," he roared as he spun around the parking lot with Jazzabelle in complete control. Jeff, disappointing as a sharpshooter, shouted repeatedly for Lyle, now soaked with Sprite, to duck down. Annie started to cry from all the noise.

I stopped the car and jumped out, disgusted at the poor performances from the very people I had counted on. "This is ridiculous!" I huffed. Lyle, Jeff, and Annie all glared at me. They blame me for this mess, I thought! Of all the nerve! I pried the leash from Lyle's hand and unwound him, leaving him dizzy and reeling. Then I stomped off with Jazzabelle, the only member of my family I was speaking to.

Jazz had a wonderful time barking and chasing cars as we walked home. I had a pretty good time myself, just walking and finding my sense of humor again. After all, strolling with the one you love on a beautiful spring day gets life back into perspective.

And if you happen to be wearing a Lone Ranger mask as you walk, so much the better.

March 1993

Random Thoughts

Changes
Lyle accuses me of still mourning for every house I've ever left. He's right. As I move into a new place, I can't help but think of all the good times I'm leaving behind. For me, every change is at best bittersweet.

The ranch hands gave Stew Ball his name because of the cowboy song, "Stew Ball Was a Race Horse." This is an example of ranch-hand humor.

Hi Ho, Stew Ball

I love Chicago — the noises, the smells, even the traffic congestion feels right to me. So what was I doing at the Don K Ranch amidst mile after uninhabited mile of Colorado mountains? I was impersonating a cowgirl — much to the amusement of my husband Lyle and our two youngest kids. Me ride a horse? I had never been more out of my element in my entire life.

Billy Crystal's character in *City Slickers* has nothing on me, I thought as I scanned the assignment list of riders and horses for the week. Lyle had Goliath, surely a steed of strength. Jeff had Clint, straightforward and reliable. Annie had Cassidy, sounding no-nonsense and noble.

Then I saw my name . . . and my horse's: Marie and . . . Stew Ball?!!! What kind of horse gets a name like that? I looked for one with a fake arrow through his head a rubber chicken strapped to his saddle bags.

Stew Ball turned out to be a sweet, red horse with two outstanding traits. The first was his size. Stew Ball was huge! He was so big that from my first ride to my last, I had a devil of a time mounting him!

This daily ritual always drew quite a crowd at the Don K. The cook came out of the kitchen to watch, wiping his hands on his apron, bacon abandoned. The Hole-in-the-Wall shopkeeper stepped out on his porch, shielding his eyes from the brilliant southwest sun, screen door slamming behind him. Squirrels showed up at just the right moment — each day in greater numbers. Every rider and every horse within view stopped whatever he was doing and watched.

First I'd put my left foot into the stirrup. Then, for what seemed like ten or twelve hours, I'd hop on my right foot while trying to swing my leg over Stew Ball's broad back. Meanwhile, everyone on the ranch — both human and animal — focused on my behind. My ample bottom bounced, waved, swayed, and bobbed like some attention-starved actor in a second-rate farce.

When I could stand it no longer, I'd find Lyle in the crowd and look at him as pathetically as possible — which was pretty easy under the circumstances. Lyle would then step up, plant his two hands firmly across my bottom, and give me a hearty shove. Once I was on Stew Ball, the crowd would disperse, and I would be off for my ride.

Which leads to Stew Ball's second outstanding trait: his speed. He was S-L-O-W . . . when he was in a hurry. When he wasn't rushing, he was S-L-O-O-O-O-O-W. Other riders took to chanting "Stew Ball, Stew Ball, Stew Ball" when we neared — to inspire him to keep moving. Sometimes, moseying along a mountain trail, I truly believe he fell asleep. He'd stumble, then look around just the way I do when I'm awakened from a nap, and finally get going again . . . at a snail's pace.

But Stew Ball's pace was never more apparent than at the final event of the week: the rodeo. Yes, buckaroos, despite our girth (Stew Ball's and mine) and our slowness, we entered the barrel race. Halfway through, I was laughing so hard I thought I would fall off! The grandstand crowd of wranglers, new friends, and family was on its feet laughing right with me and screaming, "STEW BALL, STEW BALL, STEW BALL" as we rounded the last barrel. While others completed the course in thirteen to twenty-seven seconds, Stew Ball and I took one minute forty-eight.

I've got to admit I had a ball at the dude ranch. In fact, I'll probably do it again. Odds are I'll need help getting on my horse, my big bottom will wave in the breeze, and I'll be last in the rodeo once more. Well, so be it. As we say in Chicago, that's life in the big city . . . and home on the range, too. Ride 'em , cowgirls!

March 1994

A Perfect Christmas

Three Christmases ago, my six-year-old daughter Annie was bitten in her face by a friend's dog. Let me tell you quickly that no nerves or muscles were injured. Although a scar remains, it has faded considerably.

I don't want to dwell on the details of the accident. We rushed Annie to a nearby hospital and stitches were required both inside her mouth and around her lip. A parent's nightmare. And on Christmas Day.

I wish I could tell you Christmas wasn't spoiled that year. I wish I could say that once I knew there was no functional damage to Annie's mouth I said, "Okay, everybody, let's count our blessings. Annie's face still works just fine, so let's get this in perspective and have a nice Christmas."

I wish I could say my faith was immediately deepened by this event. That I gathered my family together and lead them in thankful prayer for all our kids who were unbitten, unstitched, and untraumatized. That I knew instinctively everything would work out.

But that's not the way it went. Oh, I was calm and effective while we got help for Annie. Then when all the children were asleep and I was alone with my husband, I exploded. I burst out in punch-the-wall anger — at God and the unfairness of life and the rotten string of coincidences that led to this accident.

And I cried. Our perfect little girl. Our blithe sprit. Our baby. Annie had always wanted to be an actress. Would this accident change the course of her life? Surely it was my responsibility to prevent such things from happening. Was I a bad mother?

By December 26, Annie was feeling much better. By the 27th, Annie was playing with friends and eating solids. By the 28th, her life was mostly back to normal. In the broadest sense, Annie was already healed.

But old bodies like mine heal more slowly. Week after week, month after month, I carried around my anger and hurt.

Then one day, as I watched Annie play with our dog Jazzabelle, it struck me that the dog bite never dampened her love of animals. She enjoys them as much as before, I thought. And people. And new experiences. Annie loves them all. She has a good heart, and she lives life more fully than ever.

I looked at her closely as she played. When she smiles — which Annie does often — her scar blends into her cute little grin. It's absorbed into the whole of her. It's there all right, but it's overpowered by her sparkling eyes and warm smile.

Right then, I realized how blessed our family had been . . . and for the first time in months, my pain was lifted.

I'll never forget that Christmas. It was certainly one of the most trying days I've ever had, but ultimately it deepened my faith like few things in life have done. Looking back, I wouldn't change one minute of it. Like each of the days God makes for us, it was perfect.

Annie is still doing fine. She's so solid. Whatever she wants to be in life, nothing will keep her from it. You see, the dog bite never touched the real Annie.

And the surface scratches? Truly. They aren't important.

November 1994

Hurry Up and Die

For many years, I was an ardent follower of a philosophy which I recently came to call "The Hurry-Up-and-Die Way of Life."

I began this way of life when I was in my late teens. Even though I hadn't completed my college education, I felt pressed to hurry up and get married. Next I had to hurry up and buy a house, hurry up and start a family, hurry up and buy a bigger house in the suburbs, hurry up and own two cars, hurry up and start the kids in dance class.

And then . . . I don't quite recall just when this struck me . . . I realized I was in one mighty big hurry. What was I hurrying for? Hurrying to grow up. Hurrying to settle down. Hurrying to get old. I was racing my way through life! Why? So I could hurry up and die?!

I had no time to "enjoy." Never did I allow for savoring the present. I was too busy rushing into the future!

I've changed my approach.

Take Annie's pending birth. Years ago I would have spent my time wishing she'd arrive. But pregnancy is such a brief and special time, it deserves being appreciated for itself. Time will pass and Annie will be here, but the pregnancy will be over. Instead of rushing through it (or wishing I could), I've learned to delight in the tummy flutters, and the expanding girth (yes, even that), and nature's way of causing me to adjust my locomotion to snail-speed-ahead. In other words, to relish where Annie and I are *today*.

I try to do that with the rest of my family, too . . . enjoy them for where they are now, not what I hope they'll be tomorrow or what I'm convinced they'll someday become. I enjoy the four-year-oldness of Jeff and the twelve-year-oldness of Ed, and I try not to rush any of the kids into the next phase of life.

And you know what? Savoring life makes it much richer than "hurry up and die." I feel as if I accomplish more. I feel younger. I find more delight in life.

I like taking time to truly appreciate each day, each person, each experience . . . to take life the long way around. I've learned to "slow down and live." And I love it!

June 1985

Hip, Hip, Boo!

Spring is here and I'm scared. I'm not worried that the Cubs will look bad at their first home game or I won't be able to squeeze spring cleaning into my already stuffed schedule. Spring heightens my awareness of my weight — or more precisely my hips — and I'M PANICKY ABOUT THE WAY I'LL LOOK IN A SWIM SUIT!

My mother had these tiny, tiny hips. A HUGE APPETITE and tiny hips! What a marvelous combination she inherited from her English and Norwegian ancestors. But fate, with its twisted sense of humor, gave me my mother's appetite genes — and hip genes from my father's German forefathers! (Pass the Wiener schnitzel and potatoes, please. On second thought, just smear them across my hips. That's where they'll end up anyway!)

With the vernal equinox, weight loss becomes my top priority. I tally calories and I count fat grams. I make up weekly menus. I follow diets comprised of health foods guaranteed to take off ten pounds in ten minutes. So what's the result? Most days I spend the hours between three p.m. and dinner writing rap music in my mind – to go with the rhythm of my growling stomach.

But there's no visible change in me. I add exercise to my routine. Walking. Taking the stairs instead of the elevator. Parking at the far end of the supermarket lot. Practicing calisthenics from a magazine article entitled, "How to Lose 2 Inches in Your Hips in One Month." But I want to lose 14 inches in my hips! How many decades of lifting legs is that going to take?!!

In winter, chubby bodies are concealed by bulky clothing. The layered look. Heavy coats. Woolen tunic jackets. I dress for winter as long as I can, but there's always one warm day in late spring when I sense if I wear a down coat I'll be locked up . . . and we all know how fattening institutional food is!

So I carefully select clothing that slenderizes: the A-line skirt, the empire, the gathered waist. A bright neck scarf or a pair of dazzling earrings is a good diversion. (I have a drawer filled with brightly colored scarves purchased immediately after seeing myself in white slacks for the first time each spring.)

The dieting, the exercise, the careful dressing all help somewhat. Still, I retain these ample hip bones, obvious no matter how little flesh I lay on top of them.

But this spring I'm enlightened: I've realized that I am not my hips. In fact, my body is not my hips. My body is my toes (very, very cute toes), my smile (richer with the years), my hands (ready to comfort, eager to applaud), and all the other wonderful parts God gives each of us . . . plus all the stuff inside me which ain't half bad.

I had to live almost fifty years to understand that! But now I do, and I say, "Hello, Spring! Great to meet up with you again," and let it go at that.

You see, at long last, I really am hip.

May 1992

Frozen Christmas Dinner

My mother died in May. This Christmas, for the first time in my life, she and I won't have Christmas dinner together. Lyle and I will hold Christmas at our house, but no one will be able to enjoy Hazel's delicious candied sweet potatoes, her corny "knock-knock" jokes we always groaned at but loved, or her wonderful singing as she helped with the dishes. Without her, Christmas dinners will never be the same.

But what if Christmas dinners *could* be the same? What if we could *freeze* our favorite Christmas dinner . . . not the food but the guest list! We would compose the guest list once, and it would last forever. Year after year, we would set out our best holiday linens and silver, knowing the same well-loved guests would arrive at the appropriate time and sit at their regular places. Everything would be just as the year before. Every guest would show up . . . always.

But if Christmas guest lists were frozen, someone new couldn't be added to the table. It would already be complete. So if I had determined my ideal guest list prior to 1985 there'd be no chair for Annie, my three year old. And Dan, my niece Linda's new husband, would find no place at our Christmas meal either. Who else would be preempted from future holiday dinners because I had eliminated change?

In reality, every Christmas brings changes. Some are subtle: Annie advances from a high chair to dining room chair; Lyle's beard is a little grayer. Some are dramatic. But no two Christmases are ever the same.

Today I understand that far more than I did a year ago. There is a sense of loss that accompanies such knowledge. But there is also a keener appreciation for those who sit at my table this year . . . for the abundant blessings which remain in my life: my complex and loving husband, my eager and energetic children, my amusing and perceptive father, my friends, my family.

This Christmas will be very different for me. And in spite of that . . . perhaps because of it . . . I intend to have the most wonderful Christmas I can with the guests in attendance. After all, this is the only Christmas 1988 we'll ever have together.

I wish you a Christmas dinner with generous portions of laughter, insight, and joy. I wish you the wisdom to recognize how precious each guest at this year's banquet is. And most of all, regardless of the changes reflected at your holiday table this year, I hope you will choose to have a truly Merry Christmas.

December 1988

Flying High

I had a new experience Friday: I flew from Chicago to Cleveland with my husband. Let me rephrase that: My *husband* flew *me* from Chicago to Cleveland . . . in his plane . . . with him behind the wheel, um, the steerer thing.

Lyle's a very experienced pilot. He's been flying since he was in college and last year achieved both his instructor and commercial pilot ratings. He's flown our six kids across the country, from sea to shining sea. But . . . up until last Friday . . . Mama never flew with Papa.

Sill, I very much wanted to visit my cousin in Cleveland. At the same time, I didn't want to lose six hours driving there. So I forced back my natural uneasiness at the thought of being inside that tiny machine for a few hours and, still in possession of most of my faculties, suggested we fly to Ohio.

That's how I found myself seated next to Lyle — our two youngest, Jeff and Annie, in the back seat — heading off into the wild blue yonder.

When Lyle yelled out, "Clear left," and started the left engine, I sensed there was no turning back. By the time I heard "Clear right" and the buzz of the right engine, I knew I had quite literally turned my life over to my husband. The transfer was abrupt — as if a lever had been pulled and the moment of transfer recorded by some conscientious, interplanetary record-keeper.

For the next one and a half hours, Lyle had the responsibility of the four lives in that plane. With that load off *my* mind, you would think I could just relax and enjoy the scenery, right? I did do some of that, and it was a clear, crisp, beautiful day for doing it! The flight itself was exciting, and all my senses were alerted to what I was experiencing. Having decided to risk my life, I felt very much alive! At the same time, the experience was so different from any others I've had, I felt somewhat uneasy throughout.

Did I enjoy flying in that little plane enough to do it again? Well, I didn't rent a car and drive home.

All things considered, did I like the experience? I'm still not sure.

But will there be another trip for me? I think so maybe.

Am I always this decisive? Sometimes but not always.

Whether there are more trips in The Red Baron or not, I'm glad I made this one . . . if for no other reason than it was difficult for me to do! Crazy as it may sound, doing something that was hard to do made me feel terrific!

This summer, I hope you'll try something that's always scared you just a little . . . a trip in a plane, a project you've never felt ready to tackle, or a walk right into a situation that makes you a little uncomfortable. I'll bet it will make you feel wonderful!

July 1989

The Shopping-Cart Pledge

My mother used the phrase "sweating bullets" when she spent four hours doing laundry with the wringer washer. I use it when I exercise more than two minutes on the Cross-Country Conditioner.

I hate that machine. As I drove to the gym for a Saturday early-bird workout, I hoped there'd be an "Out of Order" sign on it — or maybe an ice cream machine or cappuccino bar had replaced it.

No such luck. There it was, waiting for me at the top of the stairs, in tip-top order. Some poor man, dripping wet, had just completed his torture session on it. As he left, he wiped the seat, the poles, and the front bar with his towel. It looked like new, and my workout was more pleasant because of that man's thoughtfulness. When I finished, I followed his example and wiped the machine down for the next exerciser. I felt pretty good as I drove to the supermarket.

After five swings through the lot, I still hadn't found a parking place. (Is there a worse time to grocery shop than Saturday at 10 a.m?!!) Then I spotted an open space in the next lane. This was turning into a great morning, I thought as I raced over there — only to discover an abandoned shopping cart sitting in the middle of my precious find! Now I was annoyed.

I got out of the car, shoved the cart out of the way, got back in the car, and finally parked. I didn't have time for this! I was certainly as busy as the next shopper, and here I was taking care of someone else's work!

I was still steaming as I walked to the store. I stopped one shopper and reminded her to please put her cart in the holder. As I flagged down another who undoubtedly needed coaching, I stopped myself cold. No matter how many people I enlightened, sooner or later I was certain to encounter an unreturned cart in a parking space. I couldn't right the wrongs of the world by changing others. I could improve things only by changing my own attitude — and trying to make things a little better for the next guy.

Right then and there, I took The Shopping-Cart Pledge. I promised myself I would always return my cart to the holder . . . and let my crusade go at that.

Since then, I've learned a few things about keeping this pledge. I've learned it's hard, even for the most well-intentioned. Some shopping days it's not just raining, it's *pouring* . . . and I'm running late . . . and I have to go the bathroom desperately. The last thing I want to do is take another thirty seconds and run that cart up to the stand.

I've learned it gets easier. Once past the first reluctant return, subsequent difficult returns became easier. I no longer *decide* each time if I will or won't return the cart. I just do it.

I've learned (silly as this may sound) that I'm happier when I return my shopping cart. I feel like I'm a real contributor to life. More in control. Less subject to life's vagaries. Sort of proud of myself. More at peace.

And I've learned that others really do watch what we do. Whether we know it or not, each of us is an example for the next guy. Through our behavior, we each set standards, and those standards spread. I've seen people watch me return my cart and then go out of their way to return theirs. Not every time, mind you. And that's perfectly okay, too, because it will always be *my* behavior and attitude I have the most impact on.

Maybe in reality this is the most any of us can do — take one or two small steps to shape the world into what we wish it were. Set an example. Live the way we want life to be. As Anne Frank wrote, "How wonderful it is that nobody need wait a single moment before starting to improve the world"

— and in the process make each Saturday morning a little sweeter.

April 1995

Random Thoughts

Little Improvements
I like to write with a wooden pencil. The pencil sharpener is at the other end of the office, so most of the time my memos look as if they were written with a lead crayon. Last month, Julie made a brilliant suggestion: Buy yourself a personal pencil sharpener.

Changed my life, that pencil sharpener did. Well, as least my attitude. I feel sharper myself . . . more in control. . . better organized. Isn't that silly! But that minor purchase worked that way. Now I'm on the lookout for other simple solutions to little frustrations: an extension cord for my hair dryer, a brighter bulb in my bedside lamp. Little by little, I'll get it all straightened out.

A Fear as Big as All Outdoors:

Chapter One

Babe in the Woods

"Please, please, please, Mom, can we go camping together?" Annie begged as she finished her cereal. "Jeff and Dad and I all love to camp, and I just know you will, too."

Camping?!! My Chicago-born-and-bred knees turned to water. I felt weak. My heart skipped a beat. Concrete, asphalt, crowds, noise, neon — they're pals of mine. I know the ropes and the sounds of the city, and I'm at ease here. But camping?

"Oh, honey, I don't know," I said. "I just don't picture myself in The Wild."

"Mom, it's not The Wild; it's the woods," Annie giggled.

"Yes, but we've all heard stories about girls being scared by wolves and chased by bears in the forest," I countered. My husband Lyle looked over the top of his newspaper. My son Jeff looked up from his favorite Saturday morning cartoon.

After a second Jeff piped in, "Right, Mom. I get it: 'Little Red Riding Hood' and 'The Three Bears'!"

"Now wait a minute," I said, over their howls of laughter, "fairy tales are often based on real life. Besides, we have no time to go now. We'd need at least a three day weekend for camping. Maybe this summer we can . . ."

"We get a four day weekend next month," Annie said. "Lincoln's birthday plus a teacher institute day."

"Yes, but," I bounced back, "we have no destination in mind."

Annie again. "We could drive to Kentucky and visit Lincoln's birthplace!" Jeff jumped out of his chair to give his sister high five.

"Yes, but," I continued, "we don't own any camping equipment. We just can't afford to buy it right now," I added, sneaking a glance at Lyle.

Silence. Just when my pulse was almost back to normal, Jeff yelled, "I've got it! We can rent! There are places that'll rent us all the camping gear we need!" Jeff and Annie joined hands and jumped around in a little circle. Our dog Jazzabelle woke up and joined the merriment.

"You know, Mom," Annie said, leaving the celebration and putting her arm around me, "camping is so much fun and the food tastes so great that it's easy to eat less. I'll bet you'll lose weight camping, Mom." Have fun and lose weight at the same time? Who could resist such a campaign promise!

"Okay, okay, we can go camping," I conceded, "but there is no way I am sleeping in a tent! My head on the ground one thin woolen blanket away from ants and other crawly things! My body a canvas sheet away from mountain lions. You camping experts will just have to figure out a different way if I'm going to go camping."

Lyle said gently, "There's a motor home rental about thirty minutes from here. They're nice units. Let's just take a look, honey." He sounded like me when I say, "Let's just let the doctor take a look at your throat" or "Just let Mommy take a look at your science test grade." Consolingly, he squeezed my hand. I was doomed and I knew it.

The next day, we looked at the biggest and best motor home available — refrigerator/freezer, microwave oven, all the conveniences. The *pièce de résistance* was a totally modern and complete bathroom. "The shower looks great, but how do you plug up this sink? There's no lever on the faucet," I asked, standing in the bathroom with Lyle. He picked up an old-fashioned rubber plug and stuck it into the drain. "That's awfully primitive, isn't it?" I blurted.

Two weekends later, we loaded Jeff, Annie, Jazzabelle, and about 63% of all our worldly possessions into the motor

home. "On the Road Again" played on the stereo as we
pulled out of our driveway.

I felt giddy. I'm just a babe in the woods, I said to myself. An old
babe, I'll admit, but a babe just the same. I'm roughing it for the
first time in my life, I realized as I walked to the microwave to
heat a cup of water. Then I settled back in my upholstered,
ergonomically-correct navigator chair, turned up the climate
control, and listened to Willie Nelson. Camping isn't so tough
after all, I thought as I sipped my *café au lait*.

And as I sipped, the motor home moved farther and farther and
farther away from civilization as I knew it.

May 1996

Chapter Two

Who's Afraid of the Big, Bad Woods?

As we turned off the highway, I braced myself: I was about to
become a camper.

Oh, my first time would be easier than most. We had rented a
luxury motor home, and I was traveling with experienced
outdoorsmen — my husband Lyle, our two youngest kids Jeff
and Annie, plus our dog Jazzabelle.

But I'd lived most of my life in Chicago's Wrigley Field
neighborhood — a far cry from this downstate Illinois campsite.
Although I hated to admit it, I felt kind of shaky as Lyle took us
deeper and deeper into the woods looking for just the right spot.

"Why settle for the middle of nowhere when the *unpopulated area*
of the middle of nowhere can be yours!" I said only half-joking.
After spiraling our motor home into the center of the
campgrounds, we finally arrived at our campsite — miles from

Driving around in the motor home was great fun for us all. The problems began when we turned off the engine — and the lights — for the night.

the entrance to the camp. While Lyle and the kids hooked up our water, toilet and purifier, and electricity, I stood in the doorway of the motor home, surveying the surrounding wilderness.

"Hey, guys," I said, feeling the reality of the situation close in on me, "we're completely isolated. There's *nobody* else here. No other cars, no other motor homes, *nobody!*" And certainly no FIFTY-YEAR-OLD WOMAN WHO HAS NEVER BEFORE BEEN CAMPING IN HER WHOLE LIFE, I wanted to add.

"February isn't high season for camping, Marie," Lyle chuckled. Then, sounding like a bad imitation of Hoss Cartwright, he added, "Let's get some grub and hit the hay."

In less time than I wished, we all were in bed and the lights were turned off. It was black. Pitch black. And moments later, quiet. Everyone had fallen asleep — except me.

I lay in bed — listening. Nothing to hear. I sat up and looked out the window into the blackness. Nothing to see. I lay back down and listened harder. Still nothing. I sat up and squinted until — just as I had suspected! There *was* something out there — and it moved! My heart began to pound. I strained to identify the sounds, the movements. As my eyes became accustomed to the dark, I saw things moving every place I looked! I could hear them, too! My heart raced almost as fast as my mind! There was a whole world of activity right outside our motor home!

When I could stand it no longer, I did the only sensible thing to do. "Lyle?" I whispered, shaking his shoulder, "are you awake?" No response. "Lyle, do you hear that?"

"What?" he asked, after lying there listening for a bit. "Do I hear what?"

"I think there are animals out there."
"Of course there are animals out there! This is the woods!"

"Yes, but I mean *scary* animals. Bears! Mountain lions! Mice!"

Lyle was good. No, Lyle was *very* good. He talked with me

patiently for a remarkably long time — the way he does when one of our kids has a nightmare. But Lyle is also human.

The second time I woke him up Lyle was about half good and half human.

The third time I awoke him Lyle was altogether human. Though he never actually yelled at me, no one would have mistaken him for Ozzie Nelson as he ripped out our hook-ups for electricity, toilet, and water. Grumbling under his breath, he climbed into the driver's seat, slammed the door, and, after thirteen right turns, drove our motor home out of the campground and onto the highway — at one fifteen in the morning.

We spent the night in a truck stop between two eighteen wheelers with their engines running.

The drone of the truck engines and lights from the parking lot relaxed me immediately. I was relieved and happy to be out of the woods. There was no mistaking that Lyle was already mightily annoyed at me. In the morning, Jeff and Annie would be disappointed when they saw where we were.

Come the dawn, I knew there would be no happy campers in this motor home. Fiddle-dee-dee, I said to myself as I scrunched up my pillow and enjoyed the perfume of the diesel engines, I'll think about that tomorrow.

And in no time, I was sleeping like a baby.

July 1996

Chapter Three

Lost in the Woods

The first dawn on the first morning of our first family camping trip. A dawn none of us — my husband Lyle, our two youngest kids Jeff and Annie, me, or even our dog Jazzabelle — would soon forget.

Although we had set up our motor home in an isolated, woodsy campground for our first night, our first morning we were not awakened by the sounds of silence: a countryside symphony of chirping birds, prancing deer, and a babbling brook. No, we were awakened by truck horns, truck air brakes, and truck engines.

You see, after everyone else was asleep that first night, I heard noises outside. Scary noises. Noises this city-slicker couldn't identify. My fears grew. My heart raced. By 2 A.M. I was experiencing an aerobic workout just by exercising my imagination. When I could stand it no longer, I insisted Lyle uproot us and find a new campsite with "friendlier" sounds: a truck stop.

The truck traffic woke Annie first. She had a lot of questions, questions like, "Why do you like the sound of trucks more than the sounds God put in the woods, Mommy?"

Then Jeff woke up. He looked out the motor home window, turned to me with a look of comprehension coming over his face, and said, "Oh, Mom, couldn't you have made it through just one night?"

Jazzabelle, following Sheltie Rule #1 ("Always bark at and chase every moving vehicle within a half mile of your tail"), had what I can only guess was the best morning of her life. She ran up and down that motor home hundreds of times, barking like crazy, as the trucks surrounding us jockeyed for position on their way out of the truck stop.

Lyle, following the old "get back on the horse" philosophy, drove us back to our original campsite for breakfast. Afterwards, the kids and Jazz ran around outside, enjoying the empty, open space.

I watched them romp as I dried the dishes. They all love it here, I thought, except me. The wide open spaces regenerates them. It leaves me uneasy.

I'm a city gal. I know nothing about the outdoors. I have zero experience. I have no circuits in my brain about forest living, no cerebral patterns for enjoying a day in nature, nothing I can build on.

I'm at a total loss in the wilderness. I'm lost in the woods. The spirit is willing but the flesh is scared stiff! And now I've ruined our trip. My eyes filled with tears.

Lyle came up behind me and slipped his arm around my waist. "Don't feel bad, Marie. The kids don't care where they *sleep*; they just want to be here in the *morning*. Are you comfortable with that?" I shook my head yes. "Well, then we have a plan: We'll spend our nights at truck stops and drive someplace scenic for our days." Lyle wiped away my tears with the corner of the dish towel.

The second night we slept in another truck stop.

The third night we slept in a campground. There was quite a celebration at breakfast the next morning. Candles (from who knows where) in my pancakes!

I will never be voted Nature Woman of the Year. I'll never have the unselfconscious ease my kids and husband do outdoors. And I'll never put camping at the top of my list of Ideal Vacations.

But I've learned there's lots I can accomplish when I'm properly motivated. And a patient husband, two flexible children, and a barking dog are highly motivating. Especially for a person like me with an underlying drive to "keep on truckin'."

September 1996

Family First

Wedding Dress Rehearsal

Because publishing craft magazines was the family business, Lyle grew up on crafting. He learned crocheting, sewing, and painting at the same time he learned baseball, music, and girls.

When I first met Lyle, I knew he was an expert crafter. Over time, I admired many of the crafts he had made, including a handsome, perfectly constructed jacket he had tailored for himself. Still, once we had decided to get married, I was momentarily shocked when he suggested he sew my wedding dress.

I had never dreamed of walking down the aisle on the most important day of my life wearing a dress made by the groom! Still, I figured this was a once-in-a-lifetime-offer — so what the heck!

When I told my junior-high daughter, Lainie, she was openly horrified. "My new stepfather is going to *make* your dress?" she asked incredulously. "Your *wedding* dress?" she continued, eyes getting bigger and bigger. "And you're going to actually *wear* it? In *church*?"

Then Lainie dropped all pretense of subtlety. "Mom, it's going to look awful. I'm going to be totally destroyed by this, I hope you know!" And the closing blow, "Why can't you just *buy* a dress like all the other *old* brides?"

Lyle and I proceeded undaunted. We selected a beautiful Vogue designer pattern and a wonderful georgette fabric in off-white. But because Lyle wanted my wedding dress absolutely perfect, he decided to make a practice dress from an old sheet. That way, he could work out his mistakes and adjust the fit on the sheet dress. The real wedding dress would be flawless.

After many late night hours in front of the sewing machine, a dozen fittings (filled with giggling), and much redoing, Lyle finally finished the sheet dress. The fit was perfect, and it looked terrific. Well, the *front* of the dress, floor length and flowing, looked terrific.

The *back* of the practice dress was another story. You see, Lyle used up all the sheet when he cut the pattern pieces. No fabric was left over. No matter! Whenever he needed new fabric to replace a mistake, he took it from the back of the dress. He started at the *bottom* of the back of the dress — cutting out a replacement sleeve here, a new pocket there — and made enough mistakes to work his way up to just below the waistband.

The back of the practice dress was so short, that from the rear I looked like I was wearing a shrunken micro-mini borrowed from some scandalously shocking rock star of the sixties! Still, Lyle and I knew the final dress would have a perfect fit and an even hem all the way around.

When Lainie came home from shopping, I showed off my completed sheet dress. "Isn't it terrific, Lainie! Look how beautifully the bodice fits," I added, pleased as punch with the trial run. "And you thought Lyle couldn't do it! See how silly you were!" I said, spinning around to give her the full effect.

Lainie stared. She staggered back a step or two, her face contorting as she began to speak: "Oh, Mother, it's much, *much* worse than I ever imagined, "she said, walking around me to get another look at the back of the dress. "The front is pretty, but . . .," she searched for the right words, ". . . the back of the dress . . . Mother, the back is . . . why, *half your behind is showing!*"

"Oh, Lainie," I laughed. "This is just a practice dress, honey. The real dress won't look this short in back, honest." I hugged her and was happy to know she was still comfortable inside my hug. Even at twelve, she was still my little girl. "It's all going to work out," I said, kissing her forehead. "You'll see. Just give it time." And I rocked her back and forth. "Our new life together will work out, too," I said, kissing her forehead and rocking her more and more until we started silly-dancing, she and I, laughing, and finally jitterbugging together.

Second marriages aren't easy. Being a stepfamily is difficult, especially at the beginning. But if one stepparent keeps a sense of humor and the other stepparent is remarkably crafty, in time all the pieces fit together just fine.

May 1990

Lainie learned the wedding dress Lyle had sewn for me turned out fine after all — and her stepfather wasn't so bad either.

Pregnant Again

Our family will experience a dramatic change sometime in May: we'll add a sixth child to our nest. And after Anne Reinke Clapper's arrival, nothing will ever be quite the same again.

(Yes, we do know it's a girl. Because I'm over 35, my doctor recommended a chromosomal test. This revealed a normal series of chromosomes — *Thank you, Dear Lord, for this blessing* — and we were advised to stock up on pink booties.)

Along with Annie come dozens of shifts for our family. Jeff (4) will gladly abandon his nickname "The Baby." Elaine (16) will no longer be sole holder of the title "Middle Child." She'll have to split that dubious distinction with Eddie (12). Susan (17) may have to adjust to sharing her room with *two* younger sisters. Scott (21) can remain quite secure that he'll retain the honor of being "Oldest Child," but he'll have a sister young enough to be his daughter!

My mom will have to add another name to her grandma apron, while my dad will have to rethink his plans for dismantling the crib kept in their extra bedroom. Lyle's folks will have the opportunity to boast about not 10 but 11 grandchildren.

And Lyle and I? We'll no longer describe our family as "A full house— three jacks and two queens." I'll have to allow an extra ten minutes to prepare for even the simplest outing with diaper-wearin' Annie. I'll have to reacquaint myself with the cat nap, every nursing mother's only hope for getting some rest those first few months.

Lyle will have to shuffle his busy work schedule to accommodate his share of trips to the pediatrician, so frequent with newborns. He'll have to brush up on the words to nursery rhymes and lullabies.

But of all the members in our family, the one who will unquestionably have the most spectacular adjustments thrust upon her is Annie herself. With her birth, she leaves behind the only "home" she's ever known . . where it was climate controlled, always serene, and fully equipped with very comfort she could want. And she'll be plunged into the sometimes outrageous, often unsettled world of the Clappers.

Still . . . I believe Annie will learn to love what she encounters in our world. I know it will take her years to adjust to all of us. I do so hope our littlest girl will have a wonderful time during that period of adjustment . . .which most of us simply call life.

March 1985

Misery Loves Equality

When our "yours, mine, and ours" family moved into its first home together, Lyle and I tried to work out room arrangements which would make everyone happy. Too many children, too few bedrooms, and all the wrong furniture made that impossible! So we set an attainable goal: Make the children equally miserable!

Our teenaged girls felt the master bedroom with attached bath should be theirs. "We spend more time in the john than the rest of the family," Susan explained.

"Plus," added Lainie, "you and Lyle are too old to need the big mirrors in the master bath."

We told them that, crazy as it might seem, old Lyle and I would be the roomies in the master bedroom. The girls would share the back bedroom with each other and the hall bath with their three brothers. They'd have the black lacquer oriental dressers, one maple bed with an E.T. bedspread, one French provincial bed with a lavender canopy, and identical toy boxes painted to look like sailing ships. Susan and Lainie were miffed.

Scott, twenty-one at the time, wanted to convert the basement family room into his own little pad. "All it needs," Scott said matter-of-factly, "is an outside entrance, a mailbox, and, of course, a fridge. I won't need an ice-maker right away."

We informed Scott he'd share an upstairs bedroom with his soon-to-be-born sister, Annie. We figured his summer work schedule and Annie's crying schedule would actually mesh quite well. Scott was crestfallen. (I believe he used the words "the most undignified room arrangement in the history of bachelorhood.")

Now Lyle and I were faced with a challenge: Jeff and Ed. They *liked* the idea of sharing a room! They didn't care if the furniture didn't match! What did they know about bathroom mirrors! So

Moments after we told our kids what their room arrangements in our new house would be, their warm smiles turned to icy glares at "the two worst parents on the planet."

how did we bring them up to the same level of misery as the others? By insisting they share the only remaining bunk we owned: a double bed.

Almost immediately, each blamed the other for stealing covers, taking the softer pillow, and drooling in his sleep. Jeff accused Ed of silent gas attacks under the blankets. Ed swore he could identify the smell of Jeff's feet on his side of the bed. In a matter of nights, they hated the room arrangement.

Mission accomplished.

In addition to treating all the kids fairly, there was one wonderful side benefit from all this: The kids got closer together. They talked for hours, sharing dreams of how nice it might have been if the rooms had been set up this way or that. They sympathized about their common misfortune at having us as their parents. As if in a single voice, they blamed Lyle and me for everything from the room arrangements to their overdue library books, bad teeth, and unrequited love. With one resounding battle-cry, they figuratively locked arms and declared us their common enemy!

We liked that, Lyle and I did. Because, you see, like most "yours, mine, and ours" families, our kids haven't spent their whole lives growing up together. They haven't had many chances to get indignant *together*. But this shared unhappiness gave them that opportunity. And sometimes parents can be very happy when their children are miserable . . . together.

October 1990

Walking Back to Basics

I've always enjoyed walking. Unfortunately, I've done very little of it lately except for the occasional trip to the corner mailbox and the all-too-frequent trek down the street to retrieve one of our late-for-dinner kids. Until the birth of our sixth child Annie, I hadn't experienced a real walk in years.

Now — partly to stave off cabin fever, partly to get my body moving again — I have daily outings with six-week-old Anne, and I've re-discovered how much I love to walk! It's a great time for me to think, observe, exercise, feel close to nature, and improve my disposition . . . not to mention what the fresh air and rocking motion of the buggy do for a baby!

Walking gives me time to sort things out in my mind. Sometimes I put my feet on automatic pilot and let my mind turn an idea over and over. At my leisure, I study that idea from every angle. Often I see with such clarity a creative response just pops into my head! I find that one of the truly amazing aspects of the mind: When we let it rip, it's very clever indeed.

When I walk I feel healthier. Oh, I'll grant you that initially my legs protested by aching, creaking, and stubbornly refusing to obey. But during the past few weeks, I've felt myself become more flexible and stronger. Now I can walk for a longer time and I move faster. I'm not going to win any walking contests, but my body simply works better.

These walks have brought back sweet memories, too. Last week Anne and I passed a house where someone was frying pork chops. The unmistakable scent transported me back thirty years to a day in the 1950's when I was thirteen.

On that particular fall afternoon, my best friend Lois and I were walking home from school down the alley between Patterson and Addison streets. We took turns naming the boys we thought were cutest. I had just finished telling her about a new boy I had seen at a church dance when I heard a wooden screen door slam. There he was! That very boy I was just telling her about, dashing down his back porch stairs! He saw us and paused. He casually waved "hi" and raced on. I staggered. My heart stopped. I felt all shivery and tingly. HE KNEW I EXISTED! And right at that moment, I smelled the pork chops his mother was cooking for dinner.

For the next few blocks as I walked with Annie, I had the pleasure of enjoying that whole scene again in my mind. Then I replayed everything I could remember about eighth grade — all prompted by the smell of the pork chops. It was one of my best walks ever.

Sometimes one of our older children joins Annie and me on our walks. They love the chance to talk with me alone without the rest of the family around. (Anne never interrupts, judges, or tells a secret, so her attendance at these chats is never resented.) And whether we're sharing secret wishes, walking along in silence, or pointing out things of interest . . . a horse chestnut tree, a perched cardinal, an unusual cloud formation . . . it's a special time together.

I'm afraid today's frantic lifestyles have put "taking a walk" in danger of extinction. But I believe walking is an art worth holding on to . . . and I hope my children will learn to enjoy it and make time for it in their lives.

How about you . . . have you *walked* your kid today?

September 1985

My Favorite Teachers

I graduated from school many years ago. Still, I am constantly learning .. mostly from my children. Each of them teaches me so much, and each has his or her own specialty. I welcome their instruction.

Scott . . . Teach me to find a happiness within myself even when faced with anger, disappointment, and hurtfulness. You don't let the moods of others influence you. You choose your state of mind, and most often that mood is "happy." Show me how.

Susan . . . Continue as a model for reaching out to people. You make friends with all sorts of wonderful children of God. You find a core of humanity in each person you meet, and you build on that core until it forms a solid friendship. I want to do that, too. Let me be your student.

Lainie . . . Keep being true to yourself. It's a joy to watch! You do it so well and make it look so easy. You look deep inside yourself and face what you see with eyes wide open. Tutor me in that art.

Eddie . . . You tackle life with unabashed vigor and determination. You triumph over problems which would halt a fainter soul. I want drive like that. Let me watch you and learn. Be my coach.

Jeff . . . Teach me by your example to thrill with the freshness in each day. There's still so much I've yet to experience. Show me how to relish life. Guide me.

Annie . . . You know the value of the moment. Even at your age, you respect the here and now. I want to enjoy today. When I do, I grow. Be my little professor. Enlighten me by your example.

How lucky each of us is who knows or lives with a young person. We can learn so much from them.

December 1983
Revised to include Annie

Children show parents what we still need to learn.

--- *Random Thoughts* ---

A Child's Vespers
Now that she's in kindergarten and all grown up, Annie has traded in "Now I Lay Me" for "The Lord's Prayer." Like many kids, she hasn't been able to understand all the language in it. (Like many kids? Who am I trying to kid! There are aspects of that prayer I'll probably ponder the rest of my life!)

Anyway, she's made two changes to the original. Near the beginning she assures God, "I will be done." And at the end, she reveals her crafting bent when she prays, "Design is the kingdom and the power and the glory." Now that's a crafter who takes her hobby seriously!

--- *Random Thoughts* ---

Another Way to Say, "I Love You"
From the time my kids could sit up, I've read to them. Cleaning, laundry, — they could wait, but reading was a must. Children learn from hearing books, newspapers, and even craft magazines read to them. They learn words, ideas, that knowledge has value, and that the reader likes the readee very, very much.

Gold Star of Courage

Annie, our first grader, was upset. As our abbreviated family ate dinner (our four oldest kids are grown and gone), Annie told her brother, her dad, and me, "Peggy doesn't like me. She calls me jerk and shrimp. I don't think she even knows my real name. She calls everybody names. She even calls herself a dork. But when she calls me names, it hurts my feelings." And with that, Annie began to cry.

We asked Annie if she had asked Peggy, a second grader, to stop. "I wrote her two notes," she offered between sniffs, "and dropped them where she sits in the lunchroom. She read them and then crumbled then up and threw them away. Yesterday's note said, 'Please stop calling me names,' and today's note said, 'If you don't stop calling me names, my big brother will beat you up.'"

Jeff almost choked on his macaroni and cheese. "Whoa! What did you say that for, Annie! I'm not going to beat up a second grade girl! I've never even been in a fight!"

Lyle and I had a suggestion: We would find Peggy's phone number in the school directory, and Annie could talk with her and try to work things out. There was just one Margaret listed in second grade, so we knew she was THE Peggy. "But her name's not Margaret, it's Peggy," Annie said. I explained that Peggy was a nickname for Margaret. Annie seemed unconvinced.

Annie hesitated as she moved to the phone. She said quietly, "I want to tell Peggy we should be friends. And I want to tell her I forgive her. That's important, I think." What perception, I thought. What depth!

Annie dialed and in seconds, Peggy herself was on the phone. Then Annie said: "Is this the person who calls herself a dork?"

Although we realized what Annie was trying to do – ascertain that she had reached the right person – Lyle, Jeff, and I were horror-stricken at her choice of words! We actually gasped!

Annie continued: "Well, this is the person who says her big brother is going to beat you up." I could have fallen off my chair! Lyle and Jeff, too! We gaped at each other in shock! I knew Annie was identifying herself to Peggy in the only way she knew. But what a beginning for negotiations!

Nevertheless, after about three minutes, they had formed a friendship pact, and Peggy was granted forgiveness. Annie hung up the phone and began dancing and jumping around the kitchen, clapping her hands and laughing, eyes filled with tears of joy.

As I cleared the dinner dishes, my eyes fell on an old box of stick-on stars. There was one star left. My dad had found it in some of my mom's belongings. She used to give our older kids a gold star whenever they did something outstanding. But by the time Annie was born, my mother was very ill, and she died when Annie was two.

"Grandma never had a chance to give Annie a star," my dad had said, "But next time Annie does something really special, give her this one."

So I did.

April 1992

Sibling Revelry

I have no brothers or sisters. I never have and I'm reasonably confident I never will. As a kid, I equated being an only-child with being a lonely child. I longed to have another child in the house. I prayed for one. I even told my parents they could use my piggy bank to buy one!

By the time I was five, I could see that my little family, wonderful as it was, wasn't nearly as exciting as Aunt Evie and Uncle Al's or Aunt Eva and Uncle How's. Their homes were filled with kids, noise, and merriment. And action! Plenty of action, day and night!

Big families have all the fun, I thought. Life with four sisters must be one constant, wonderful tea party! A big brother to protect me? That would be heavenly! A kid sister to show the ropes? I'd enjoy every second. Brothers AND sisters? A veritable smorgasbord of playtime possibilities!

Growing up alone, I never realized that life wasn't always glorious between brother and sister. That sometimes it meant getting tattled on, egged-on, and belched on. But now, as the mother of six, I know about boys and girls and the real dynamics of life in a big family.

Having a brother means spending your days with somebody who knows all the things that make you happy . . . and precisely the buttons to push to get you to fall apart. If Jeff simply puts his foot on the rung of Annie's chair in a certain fashion, she wails. Scott and Eddie once perfected a way of saying Lainie's name — guaranteed to make her break down and cry! And it doesn't take a genius to know what "Daaaad! He's looking at me!" means.

Having a sister means you are never alone . . . it also means you are NEVER alone. I've found the same to be true of having a daughter. Privacy, something I took for granted the first half of my life, has now all but disappeared from my days. Girls, at least mine, don't understand "Please leave me alone for ten minutes." Susan once walked into the bathroom while I was soaking in the tub. "But you were so quiet," she said. "you should play the radio or splash the water so I know you're in there." Right.

Girls and boys in a family make sincere efforts to do what's asked . . . if it suits their plans. I've told my kids repeatedly, "If I'm in my bathroom, please don't disturb me. This is my only hideaway." But there I was, trying to read the last chapter of a mystery novel, when I saw a note being slipped under the door. (Do you have any idea how compelling a note slipped under a door is?) The note said:

Mom,

Can I go over to Rob's house?

Your son, Ed

P.S. This doesn't count as disturbing you because I didn't knock.

Life with my six kids has certainly kept me from being lonely. Maybe they're really the brothers and sisters I prayed for when I was little. I just had to wait half my life to meet them.

My pastor says be careful what you pray for because you just might get it. I say God has a marvelous sense of humor . . . and a sense of timing that continues to amaze and delight me!

March 1992

Number Please

Whenever anyone asks me how many kids I have, I'm momentarily stumped.

Do I tell them the number of children I've raised? The number I've given birth to? The number that call me Mother? It's a tough question to answer without a census of the players, their ages, genetic charts, and a detailed family tree. ("Dim the lights and warm up the slide projector. Someone just asked Mom how many kids she has.")

You see, my husband and I were each married before. Lyle had two children from his first marriage: Scott (now 29) and Susan (25). My first husband and I adopted two: Lainie (24) and Eddie (20). And Lyle and I together have two: Jeff (12) and Annie (7). So I'm the mother of two stepkids I've cared about since they were little, two adopted kids I've raised from infancy, and two homegrown which I had when most of my friends were retiring their copies of Dr. Spock.

(I suggest you highlight the previous paragraph and dog-ear this page. That way if you forget which kid is whose or who is related to whom, you can flip back here for this ready reference. Myself, I've copied this paragraph and have it posted on my refrigerator. At my age, I need all the memory joggers I can find.)

In response to the "how many kids" question, I've answered six — the number I've helped raise — and been accused of "cheating" to come up with a bigger number than I "deserve." I've answered four — the number who call me Mother — and been given a lecture on the importance of loving your stepchildren regardless of what they call you. I've answered two — the number I've birthed — and been asked, "Do you always distinguish between your own and your adopted and step children?" What's a mother to do?!!

Over the years, I developed a reasonably simple answer: "He has two, and I have two, and we have two together." (It almost sings, doesn't it?) But I've said those same words so many times they bore me! So at a block party last year, I decided to throw out my usual answer and test a different wording. A dignified matron, new to our neighborhood, asked me about my kids. I said, "Lyle and I have six children . . . and Lyle is the father of the first two and the last two." She choked on her stuffed mushroom and coughed, "How nice." Halfway through the barbecued chicken and baked beans I realized what I had said!

But I'll confess that sometimes I intentionally have some fun with this unusual configuration of kids. At a recent wedding reception, a group of us were talking about our families. One woman I hardly knew seemed to have an insatiable curiosity about mine. She wasn't aware of how I had come to have six kids and didn't care how much each one meant to me. Just the same she asked me question after question.

In answer to one of her inquiries, I had just told her our oldest was almost thirty. She looked me up and down and sniffed, "And how old were you when you had your first?" That pushed me over the invasion-of-privacy edge.

I answered — in perfect honesty, please note —, "I was pregnant for the first time when I was thirty-seven." Hours later, that woman was still standing in the very same spot — adding, subtracting, and clucking away.

The number of kids isn't really important. I just feel really lucky to have had such rich mothering experiences and such great kids. Scott and Susan still turn to me on occasion to share their troubles and their joys. That pleases me deeply. In addition to their own wonderful mom, they have me — and I'm not through mothering them yet. They know it and I know it and we all like it that way.

Watching Lainie and Eddie, who share none of my genes, act and react as I do delights me. Lainie and I like the same books, and Eddie and I give the same looks. These two kids are mine as much as children can be anyone's. They're living affirmations of the adoption process — that miraculous joint venture of God and man.

Jeff noticed the clothes his three sisters wore and said, "Hey, I'm sitting here with full jeans (Annie wore jeans overalls), half jeans (Susan wore jeans and a shirt), and no jeans (instead of jeans, Lainie wore a dress)."

Lyle, always ready for a little pun, added, "Precisely. Annie's your full sister and shares full genes with you, Jeff. Susan's your half-sister and shares half her genes with you. And Lainie — well, we're all glad Marie adopted Lainie into this family — which means she and you share no genes, Jeff!"

And there's no denying that I get a tremendous kick out of hearing someone say Jeff has my eyes or Annie my smile — perhaps because I waited so long to reproduce! Seeing a little face that resembles mine just plain tickles me. Probably always will.

How many kids do I have? The perfect number . . . for me and for them.

May 1993

Random Thoughts

Bowled Over by Creative Accounting
Annie (the youngest bowler in our family) became so frustrated by scoring one zero frame after another that she wanted to quit. She didn't mind losing, but she felt like she wasn't even in the game!

Then Lyle had an inspiration: "Instead of scoring the number of pins you knock down, Annie, tally what you *think* you *deserve.*" With that, Annie became a real participant and family bowling was fun for all.

Sometimes we do things in the same old unsatisfactory way for no reason other than it's become routine. If your objective is simply to have fun, don't hesitate to change the rules! You're allowed.

Mystery Unsolved

Two-year-old children take firm stands on all sorts of issues. Forty-something mothers of two-year-old children usually give them a run for their money — at least that's the way things were with my daughter Annie and me the summer she turned two. Every decision became a battleground. Every day brought face-to-face combat. Every eventuality produced a winner and a loser.

That hot morning in August was no exception. Our dance of power began the moment I told Annie I thought this was the perfect day to wear her yellow and blue sundress to church. She thought about the dress for a second or two and then flatly said, "No," revealing her cause-du-jour: her clothes. The line was drawn in the sandbox.

I ordered; I cajoled; I digressed; I begged. Annie simply refused.

Finally at nine-fifty-two, we had run out of time and I had run out of patience. "What I want from you, young lady," I said humorlessly, "is obedience."

Annie, still in only diaper and undershirt, weighed this possibility once more. Then, meeting me eyeball to eyeball, she responded with equal resolve: "No-bedience, Mommy."

Just at that moment, my husband Lyle interceded. "Marie, I'll work this out with Annie. Set out the clothes you want her to wear, and we'll meet you later," he said. I was out the door in a flash.

Sitting in church, I began to get things back into perspective. She's just a child, I reminded myself. You're a mature adult, Marie; this is no contest of peers. I had to laugh at myself.

Just then, sure enough, about a quarter after ten, I saw Lyle and Annie coming down the side aisle, both of them all smiles. That's terrific, I thought. She's wearing the sundress I wanted her to wear and she's smiling! Quite an accomplishment for Daddy!

But as they came nearer, I could tell something was wrong. Somehow the dress looked weird. Very weird. As they slid into the pew next to me, I knew what the problem was: Annie's *head* was in the *armhole* of the dress! She had one arm in the other armhole and her second arm in the neck opening. The ruffled hem of the dress ran down her side like an alien's cape. The bottom of the dress was gathered like a potato sack. I had never before seen anything quite like it!

"Everything worked out fine, honey," Lyle said as he patted my hand, "but we would have been here five minutes earlier if that dress were the right size! I would never have managed if Annie hadn't cooperated."

I stared at Lyle as he flipped through a hymnal and began singing. Was he putting me on? Didn't he realize what he had done? I looked at Annie. She stopped scribbling on the Visitor Card she'd taken from the pew in front of her and blinked at me a time or two. Then she made a little kiss at me with her mouth and smiled warmly. Had I been duped by my daughter? Were the two of them in cahoots?

Nahhh . . .

That was eight years ago. I still don't know what the truth is, but does it matter? I do know that little adventure showed me the importance of keeping things in perspective and keeping my sense of humor as Annie grows up.

Now if I can only hold on to my sense of humor for another thirty years.

September 1995

Mothering Day

Once upon a time, all children lived with Mom and Dad on a sunny, tree-lined street. There was a brother or a sister or two, a dog named Spot, and a clubhouse in the yard.

No one argued . . . certainly not Mom and Dad! . . . and dinner hour was filled with pleasant conversation, piping hot meals Mom had spent all day preparing, and a recollection of Baby's antics during the day. Everyone laughed and passed the mashed potatoes please.

For many of us, that Dick and Jane world is no more. In my family, for example, living under Lyle's and my roof, is Lyle's son Scott, my son Eddie, and our son Jeff. Annie (Lyle's and my biological daughter, half sister to four on two different sides, and Jeff's sister) is a definite presence.

But our immediate family doesn't end at our property line.

Susan (Lyle's daughter, my stepdaughter, Scott's sister, Lainie and Eddie's stepsister, Annie and Jeff's half-sister) spends most of the year in another state with her mom.

And to round out our family, Lainie (my daughter, Lyle's stepdaughter, Eddie's sister, Scott and Susan's stepsister, and Annie and Jeff's half-sister) lives near us with her dad and her stepmom (who is also Eddie's stepmom and is thought of so fondly by Jeff she ought to be considered at least Jeff's half-step-mom-in-law).

Even without throwing in grandmas and grandpas, you can see this is a complicated set up . . . almost requiring a roster of players!

But today unusual family set-ups are not uncommon. Divorce, death, and a veritable smorgasbord of lifestyles have forced us to redefine the traditional way of celebrating Mother's Day. Perhaps we should begin by renaming this holiday "Mothering Day . . . the time to honor those who mother us."

If you work with a group of kids, ask each child who he lives with or who's going to get the wonderful Mother's Day gift he's making. Then help him adapt the gift so it's worded appropriately. It might be for his stepgrandmother, or his aunt, or even his dad, if that's the one who does the nurturing in his life.

Chances are 50/50 that he doesn't live in a Dick and Jane world. But with a little sensitivity from teachers and leaders close to him, every child can grow up believing his world is still pretty terrific!

March 1984
Revised to include Annie

Virtual Parenting and the Wire Monkey

Last week I read about Virtual Parenting in the *Wall Street Journal*. Virtual Parenting, which has common roots with both the word "virtue" and the concept of Virtual Reality, is a way for working parents to compensate for separation from their kids using the gadgets of this electronic age. During times of separation, for example, parents can send video or audio tapes of themselves to their children, e-mail messages, and, with the help of the fax machine, even keep tabs on homework.

As a working mom who also travels, I like these ideas. Even the somewhat outlandish suggestion to dine with your kids by speakerphone has a practicality which could help in a pinch.

But Virtual Parenting took me back thirty years to Psychology 101 and the Wire Monkey experiment.

Using only wire, a scientist made a monkey doll, then placed food and water near it inside a cage. He put a live little monkey inside the cage with the wire monkey, who became a surrogate mother of sorts to the little guy, effectively providing him with all the nourishment needed to survive.

Next, the scientist made a second wire monkey just like the first except this one he padded and covered with fabric. He put the soft monkey in its own cage with food and water, too. For several days, the baby monkey alternated between cages.

Then one day the scientist left both cage doors open. The monkey could enter either cage. Time and again, he chose the cage with the soft monkey inside.

Even when the scientist removed the food and water from the cage with the soft monkey, the baby monkey continued to choose it. I can still see that little spider monkey cuddling with the soft monkey, his spindly arms wrapped around her, his big eyes staring into the camera.

Perhaps as important as food and water, all God's creatures need to snuggle up with something soft. Maybe that's why God made grandmas. Grandmas are even fluffier than moms!

Virtual Parenting is a creative solution to a tough situation, but let's not kid ourselves. Parenting goes way beyond sending electronic messages. Maybe more than anything else, parenting is touching. Hugging. Rocking. Cuddling. Patting. Smoothing. Snuggling.

I remember being about four years old. I remember walking down Addison Street with my dad when he came back from the Philippines. All the way, my little hand was held by his. I was amazed at how large his hands were and how warm! He rubbed his thumb along my hand as he talked. I knew he was home for good.

I remember crying once when a friend had hurt my feelings. My mom, stooping down next to me on the sidewalk, brushed away the hair from my eyes and held my head in both her hands. She looked at me very intensely and talked so earnestly. I'll never forget feeling the compassion and reassurance I felt from her.

I remember a summer night sitting in my grandma's lap in the big, squeaky rocking chair. She patted my bottom in a steady rhythm and softly sang to me in Norwegian. Her robe was silky and soft against my cheek. Her hands were strong. Surely my life was overflowing with guardian angels!

Children *become* the behavior that surrounds them. They learn virtues from the feelings, the actions, and the faces — not the faxes — they read. From the touches — gentle, harsh or indifferent — of the people in their lives. There can be no electronic substitutes. Just the genuine article, conveyed through the inexplicable magic that happens whenever hand touches hand and the message, "I care about you; you are worth loving" flows from parent to child.

Virtual Parenting is an option I'm sure I'll use on occasion. But it's not my preferred method of raising kids. My favorite way isn't electronic. It's not flashy. It's just old-fashioned Hands-On Parenting. And it's what I give my little monkeys every chance I can.

March 1996

Random Thoughts

A to Z Praise

Sue, Lyle's and my assistant, realized she spent more time directing her son Russell ("Don't do that please!" "Do it this way!" "Clean your room!") than telling him she loved him. So to balance the scales a bit, she wrote him a note listing twenty-six words — from A to Z — which described Russell. She chose accurate, positive words which really fit him — like J - jovial, S - sensitive, and Z - zealous. Well, needless to say, Russell loved it! He learned a lot about both his mom and himself . . . and expanded his vocabulary to boot!

Plastic Fork Rebellions

At some point in their teens, most children rebel.

That's just what the kids at Four Corners School in Greenfield, Mass., did when they learned that their lunchroom was converting from stainless to plastic forks. Their battle cry? "School is no picnic."

The kids wrote petitions, met with school board members, and demonstrated at every turn their position on plastic forks. Eventually, a local restauranteur donated his old silverware when he bought new. The kids nearly cheered the roof off the auditorium when they heard the news.

I've survived many Plastic Fork-ish Rebellions in raising our six kids. My kids have rebelled against me and my ways by eating vegetarian diets and growing tails. They've held firm on the issue of what radio station they'll listen to. They've fought to the finish their right to leave their gym shoes untied.

Although these insurrections are annoying, I consider myself lucky . . . because as long as my kids rebel in ways like these, I know I have a decent shot at getting them through adolescence just the way I like them: alive.

Long live Plastic Fork Rebellions! Long live the Rebels!

June 1988

Baby Pictures

Does a mother ever forget what a darling each of her children was as a baby? I haven't. Oh, like most parents of six, I do get confused about which one had the measles on Halloween and which took his first step on his first birthday. (I'll never forget which one repeatedly amused himself during naptime by undoing his diaper and sculpting. I've tried to forget, mind you, but I can't.) I carry in my mind baby pictures of each of my four [(Lyle brought two almost teenagers to the party)] which will never fade.

Lainie was six weeks old when we first met. The adoption agency had her all clean and happy and set up in a special room and a special crib which I can still see these twenty-two years later. When her dad and I walked in, she heard us and looked our way immediately. When I picked her up, she broke into a smile . . . first her eyes, next her mouth, then her whole face. As a first-time mother, that smile gave me just the assurance I needed. I knew we would be lifelong friends.

I always envision my second, Eddie, very close up. I see his big brown eyes about three inches away from my blue eyes, because above all else, Eddie liked to be carried. Carried always. Carried everywhere. Carried from the first day we met until he was about two and a half years old. Because of Eddie, I am perhaps the only mother in history who could fold clothes, vacuum a floor, and peel potatoes one handed. Since 1972 my right bicep has been twice the size of my left, thanks to Ed, and I can arm wrestle with the best of them (right arms only please).

Jeff, now ten, was the only one who sucked his thumb. Once when he was a toddler, he injured his right thumb, the thumb of choice. "What can I do, Mama?" he wailed sadly. Matter of factly, I told him to suck his other thumb. He stared at his left thumb incredulously. "Suck this?" he asked in disbelief, holding up his left thumb as if I'd just suggested he suck an old car part. Until Jeff was in third grade, he would fall asleep with the comfort of this thumb. I would find him asleep on his side, his hair toussled, his breathing even and deep, his mouth slack, and his right thumb just barely touching the edge of his lip . . . as if it had fallen asleep on the job.

Annie, who's almost six, is lithe and delicate today. But when she was born, she weighed 10 pounds 5 ounces! That's a lot of baby girl! The hospital put pink knit caps on newborn girls and blue on boys. The first time Lyle and I walked to the viewing room we saw all the babies wearing their caps . . . except for Annie. She had hers lying across her chest because there just wasn't a cap big enough for her!

Babies evoke so many memories. The way they smell, the softness of their skin, the sweet little sounds they make. There's nothing in the world like them, and when you have one in your life there's nothing you wouldn't do for it.

About five years ago, Lainie may have said it best. I had asked her to walk to the store to pick up a gallon of milk. "But, Mom, a gallon of milk is so heavy," she lamented.

"Lainie, one gallon of milk weighs much less than Annie and you never complain about carrying her around," I retorted.

"But, Mother," Lainie said with that same smile I had first met years ago, "a gallon of milk can't hug back."

March 1991

Break the Rules and Make a Memory

The day my husband Lyle and our eight-year-old Jeff returned from a Florida weekend together, Jeff gave me a review of their wonderful getaway.

"And, Mom," Jeff said with a twinkle, "the last night Dad and I broke all the rules." I raised my eyebrows, waiting for more.

"We ate pizza in bed," he grinned, delighted to the bone.

Jeff's and Lyle's experience brought to mind a night in the mid-1940's when my mother and I displayed a similar disregard for proper behavior.

I was about four, and my dad was overseas in the service. My mom was feeling sad that night, so, despite the fact that it was Chicago and it was winter, we hopped on a bus and went to the movies.

While we were inside the theater, the temperature must have dropped twenty degrees. When we stepped outside, we were greeted with a howling wind and a snowstorm . . . but no bus. We waited and waited. The longer we waited, the colder we got. We tried stomping our feet and rubbing our gloved hands together to warm up, but we were still freezing!

Finally, my mother broke all the rules of proper behavior while waiting for a bus. Right in front of the world and everybody, she unbuttoned her coat, snuggled me inside, and then re-buttoned her coat around my head. My face and legs were all that remained exposed to the chill.

Several movie-goers stared. Passers-by gave us double-takes. Some people even shook their heads and clucked their tongues in disapproval. My mom giggled.

And me? I never felt so warm and so loved in my life. I didn't care if the bus ever came.

Does it get any better than being buttoned inside your mother's coat during a winter storm? Or sitting on a bed, sun-burned legs crossed, dressed in underpants, eating cheese and sausage pizza . . . just you and your dad? Does it ever get any better than that?

September 1988

Random Thoughts

When You Care Enough to Disregard the Rules
Years ago, my son Eddie, about four at the time, bought Grandpa's birthday card all by himself. It started off, "Happy Valentine's Day to the Woman I Love." My dad said he was glad the card was hand-delivered because he would have had a devil of a time figuring out who had sent it!

I asked Eddie why he had chosen that card. He said the picture on the front was beautiful, and that the card would make Grandpa very happy. Eddie was right.

Year after year I find myself thinking how lucky I am to live my life among such sages, my offspring.

Brotherly Love

Almost from his beginning, Jeff wanted a baby sister. Finally, after waiting three days short of five years, he got his wish . . . Annie was born.

My husband Lyle and I knew immediately that they would be fast friends. The age difference brought sibling rivalry to a minimum. And the fact that friends, relatives, and even strangers commented on how much they looked alike didn't hurt either!

During Jeff and Annie's first two-and-a-half years together, Lyle and I watched them roughhouse like cub lions. We saw Annie burst into tears if Jeff was punished. We melted when Jeff voluntarily gave Annie the last raisin in the box, his favorite car to play with, the softer pillow to nap on.

One evening a few weeks back, Jeff and I were sitting on the couch. I was reading, absorbed. He apparently was doing some heavy-duty life-planning.

"Mom," he asked quietly, "can somebody marry his sister?"

Without removing my eyes from the pages of my book, I launched into an explanation of western culture, the genetic complications of inter-family marriages, and practices of native tribes in Bora Bora. Then all of a sudden I realized what Jeff's real question was!

"Jeff, you really love Annie a lot, don't you."

He nodded yes readily and seemed relieved that I understood. "She's so cute, Mom! She's sweet and she's fun . . . and when I'm tired, she rubs my feet." (That'd do it for me right there, I can assure you!)

"I can see how you might think about marrying her, Jeff. But one day, honey, you'll meet a girl and you'll think to yourself,

Jeff has shepherded Annie through church Christmas pageants, nourished her, and answered her questions about American history and boys.

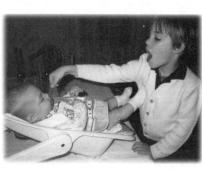

'There's something about her that I really like.' She'll remind you in some way of Annie. Maybe she'll be blond and sweet. Or maybe she'll wrinkle up her nose when she giggles. Or maybe she'll put a pair of underpants on her head and imitate a bunny rabbit."

We both laughed, picturing Annie's favorite way of amusing the family.

"But, Jeff, " I said, pulling him closer, "someday you'll find a girl just as wonderful as Annie. And you'll be a fine husband for her. I know that because you're a terrific brother for Annie."

A single tear rolled down his cheek. He sighed. He paused. Then, "I'm going to see if Mike and Rob can play baseball." And he was out the door in seconds.

Some things never change. Spring. Love. And the Great American Pastime.

March 1988

Just Us Girls

Mama's Crowning Glory

I was six years old when I had my worst hair day ever — and it wasn't even my own hair.

That day, I was delighted to discover my mother resting on the couch — delighted because that meant I could brush and comb her hair.

My mother's hair was remarkable — shoulder-length, thick, auburn — very different from my blond, thin, wispy curls. Everyone commented on its beauty, and even my mother, who was usually very humble, referred to her hair as her "crowning glory." I felt honored indeed that she allowed me to sometimes be her hairdresser.

I brushed her hair tenderly with her big wooden brush with the natural bristles. Even after she had drifted off to sleep, I kept brushing. Her hair was so shiny and smooth. I loved the way it looked and felt after the brush ran through it. I was fascinated by the way the hairs kept their position after I combed them, making little lanes where the comb teeth had traveled.

Hair this lovely must be very rare, I thought . . . and began pretending I was a famous hair artist allowed to create the world's greatest hair-do.

With utmost care, I combed to the ends of my mother's hair. Then, inspired, I neatly and carefully flipped the comb over, winding my mother's hair around the comb. I liked that. I patted any stray hairs into obedience. When every hair was in place, I turned the comb again, winding the hair tightly. I rolled the comb over and over until that entire section of her hair was all wound around the comb all the way up to her scalp. Then, just for good measure, I gave the comb one last turn. There. I had wound the comb into her hair completely.

I studied my masterpiece. Perfect, I thought. The comb looks like a little bird perched on the edge of my mother's forehead. Then I decided to design something else . . . but the comb wouldn't budge.

The more I tried to loosen it, the more firmly set it became. My heart started to pound. I felt dizzy. The comb seemed glued to my mother's scalp! I wiggled it and picked at it and tried everything I could think of, but the comb just wouldn't come out!

I felt a suffocating panic and I let out a howl that made my mother jump out of her sleep. She sat bolt upright on the couch, the tortoise-shell comb plastered against the left side of her forehead.

"Mommy!" I cried. "I ruined your crowning glory!"

She stared at me half a second, then reached up and felt the comb. Almost instantly, she figured out what had happened.

She was mad. She never yelled, she never cried, but I knew.

Both of us scurried around the apartment — me whimpering the whole time — trying desperately to remove the comb.

But finally, we abandoned all hope. My mother took out the scissors and cut the comb out of her hair. Where her bangs should have been was just a patch of auburn stubble with a bald spot in the center.

I had never felt worse in my whole little life. "Oh, Mama, I'm so sorry," I sobbed.

She took a long, slow breath and then said, "It'll grow back, honey. All we have to do is wait." She dried my tears with her hanky and kissed me and kissed me all over my face. Then she hugged me and rocked me until I knew she would surely always love me no matter what.

After all these years, I still think of that bad hair day. It became my first of many lessons in patience . . . and a never-to-be forgotten picture of grace — my mother's true crowning glory.

May 1995

Random Thoughts

Coming of Age
Annie must have felt left out when her big sis Lainie came home for a visit and spent most of her time talking with me about recipes, decorating, and ways to juggle college and household. Clearly, we were engaged in "woman talk."

But clever six-year-old that she is, Annie thought of credentials to maintain her status. "I know how to do needlepoint now, Lainie," boasted Annie. Then, to cement her position, she added, "And I drink tea."

Breaking the Stepmother Barrier

Because I'm the publisher of craft magazines, people expect me to be a great crafter. I'm really not.

I enjoy crafts but I work (how can I phrase this without being unkind to myself?) slowly. Very slowly. Like the cross-stitch plaque I've been working on for my husband Lyle's 40th birthday. This April he'll be 48. (See what I mean.) Still, crafting has helped me in one of the most important roles of my life: as a stepmother.

When Lyle and I married, his son Scott was fifteen. Scott and I were fast friends. We both love music, so I played my old Ella Fitzgerald records for him, and he introduced me to groups whose names and sounds I still find unintelligible. Before either of us knew what was happening, we trusted each other enough to yell and to hug.

But Lyle's twelve-year-old daughter Susan? That was another story. It wasn't as if Susan and I didn't like each other. We did. But the harder we tried to be at ease with each other, the more self-conscious we became.

Then one Saturday morning, Susan saw me working on my cross-stitch. She was interested, so I showed her the basic stitch. She liked it. That afternoon I got her started, and we sat on the porch glider, sipping lemonade, working on our projects in silence and occasionally talking about this or that.

Because she was learning, she sat near me. Because I was teaching her needlecraft, our hands sometimes touched and our eyes often met. Because she is Susan, we giggled.

As the day wore on, Susan and I became more engrossed in our needlework than ourselves, and we loosened up. One stitch at a time, we felt comfortable enough to show each other the real person wielding the embroidery needle.

*Susan and I have an ease and trust with
each other that didn't begin until years after
we became stepdaughter and stepmother.*

After dinner, we moved inside and cross-stitched and talked until bedtime. (I found out later that Susan stayed up stitching until two-thirty!) As the summer passed, Susan and I spent time together pouring over craft magazines and needlepoint catalogs, planning projects, exchanging pointers . . . and simply getting to know each other.

That was eight years ago. Today Susan is a good friend of mine . . . and a cross-stitch whiz! This year she began designing her own cross-stitch pieces. Unlike me, Susan is naturally neat and orderly. She can display her work, back or front. Both views are lovely, mathematical pieces of magic which deserve the kind of pride she has in them.

And where have I gone with my cross-stitch in this same period? Well, I still frame and add a backing to each piece as soon as the last stitch is sewn. That way I avoid the humiliation of having some curious innocent turn over my work only to see my tangled, snarled, gnarled mess.

But more important than the handicraft itself, cross-stitch became the point of entry for a real relationship. Susan and I talk the language of cross-stitch. It doesn't matter that I speak it with a bad accent and she's learned the king's cross-stitch. We've discovered a common love . . . in addition to her dad!

I doubt if I'll ever be a great crafter. But I know if I really knuckle down with that birthday piece I've been working on so long, I can make Susan's daddy real happy this April. On the other hand, if Susan helps me make just one or two design changes, I'll bet I can modify that plaque to commemorate Lyle's fiftieth!

February 1989

Yellow Rose

Yesterday as I drove to work, I heard "Yellow Rose of Texas" on the radio. Just hearing that song sent a shiver down my spine. When I was in junior high, that was the record that was always played while the boys chose their dance partners.

We girls stood on a painted green line on the gym floor, backs to the boys. The boys lined up across the gym on a painted red line . . . in sprint position. When everyone was reasonably quiet (fear put me into a state of semi-conscious in a matter of seconds), Mr. Frazier, the gym teacher, blew his whistle, and the boys were off. Each was supposed to calmly walk to the partner of his choice and stand behind her. When all of us were matched up, each boy was to tap his partner on the shoulder, make light conversation with her until the actual dance record began, and then glide away.

It never quite worked out like that.

Almost before the whistle reached Mr. Frazier's lips, each boy pushed, kicked, and beelined his way to Lori Rodgers. I couldn't see what was actually going on, but I knew no one was standing behind me. Twenty-four boys were behind Lori. I could tell by the noise at the "short" end of the line. (Yes, to make it even more frightful, we girls had to line up according to height. I was fifth from the tallest at the start of 7th grade and worked my way to second tallest by the end of 8th.)

Then, with "Yellow Rose of Texas" playing all the while, Mr. Frazier would demand that some of the boys move to other girls. Only those boys with the weakest of constitutions would relent. Next Mr. Frazier would blow his whistle repeatedly . . . with little or no effect. Finally he'd go over to the pile of pulsating pubescence standing behind Lori and catapult each boy in one direction or the other, shouting out that boy's Lori-replacement. Sometimes there was so much reluctance by the boys that Mr. Frazier had to play "Yellow Rose of Texas" a second time!

Of all the painful times in junior high, those dance classes were the worst. I never felt less special in my life. Who could ever want me?! I was tall, skinny . . . and unsure of myself.

Today one of those descriptives still applies. But during these thirty years, I've learned to accept myself for the person I am, and that self-acceptance makes all the difference in the world.

Maybe years ago that was the quality Lori Rodgers had which made her so popular. Even as a thirteen-year-old, she knew who she was. Everybody around her felt that sureness and wanted to be near it, thinking some might rub off. Maybe Lori knew even then that as the only person in the world quite like herself she was indeed a beautiful flower, a sort of rose.

I hope you too remember that you are one-of-a-kind. Celebrate the music, the rhythm, every note of being you . . . even if at this time there is no one standing behind you ready to tap you on the shoulder and join you in that special dance.

May 1989

Last Start

This fall the youngest of our six children starts kindergarten. What a memorable time that is! I still can recall my first day in school even though it was (is this possible?) over forty years ago.

Miss Flynn smelled like lily of the valley, my favorite flower. As I walked in, she pointed toward one end of the room and told me to put my things in the cloak room. There's a special room here just for *cloaks*, I thought as I hung up my woolen sweater. I wondered how many kids would be wearing cloaks.

I sat on the red circle painted on the oak floor - hands folded, lips silent — waiting to begin. First I couldn't hold back a great big grin, and then my chin quivered as I fought back tears. I was bursting with eagerness and fear and awe!

I looked around at the bright pictures on the walls and the kids who looked much like me. Kindergarten was going to be a wonderful place to spend my mornings, I decided.

In no time at all, each of us was busy. A girl in braids ate a green crayon and a side dish of paste. Some sorry soul became so absorbed in washing the dishes in the play kitchen that she forgot to allow time to get to the washroom. A boy in suspenders and bow tie dressed up as a bride . . . high heels, gown, veil . . . and looked simply stunning.

I played with building blocks until snacktime: two butter cookies and my very own glass bottle of whole milk.

When the morning ended, I raced out of school — as proud of myself as I had ever been! And there to meet me was my mom — as proud of me as I was!

Now my last child starts kindergarten. But there will be no cloak room for Annie. She'll hang her neon-pink windbreaker in her own locker. She'll probably work on the school computer some time during the day. And her snack will be a nutritious one like cream cheese and wheat germ on celery stalks washed down with cran-apple juice.

But the day will still be electrifying for her. She'll love her teacher before attendance is even taken. The room will smell of the sweet breath of children and soap and young skin moist with anticipation. Annie will be enthralled with it all.

And when she rushes out at the end of that first morning, I'll be waiting at the door by the playground just as my mom was. Oh, I'll have skipped my noontime workout, and I'll have my secretary handling my calls while I'm out of the office . . . but I'll be there.

Because I know when that dismissal bell rings, I'm in for one of the sweetest pleasures in life: walking home, hand-in-hand, with my favorite five-year-old in the whole world on her first day of school. And that, my friend, is an experience I shall savor . . . one last time.

September 1990

Random Thoughts

School Report
After Annie's first day in kindergarten, I met her as planned. She squealed, we hugged, and then we started our walk home. When I asked her how things had gone, she stopped walking and looked at me. "Mom," she said with complete sincerity, "it was the greatest day of my life."

Gee. I hope it isn't all down hill from here!

Bosom Buddies

Lois and I have been friends from the beginning. Years ago, when Lois' Mom brought home her little bundle of joy, I was crawling around and sucking my thumb just one floor up.

(Yes, Lois is younger. But I like to think that my extra year gives me a greater air of maturity. It's okay if you won't buy that idea. Almost no one does.)

Lois and I have shared some crazy times during the 40+ years of our friendship. When we were nine and ten and the Chicago heat became intolerable, we would walk to the only air-conditioned spot in our neighborhood, Sears Roebuck. We would head straight for the furniture department, select a comfortable couch which had a panoramic view of the third floor, and begin the work we had come there to do: pretend.

We would pretend that she and I were orphans who owned this particular Sears Roebuck. We lived on the top floor with our pets and servants. How would we arrange the furnishings? How would we keep shoppers out of our "home"? Would we put the bathroom near the escalator or near the water fountain? What would we bring up from floors one and two? Where would we do our homework? Would we watch all the TVs at one time? These were questions we tackled with delight, sometimes disagreeing over an answer, sometimes lingering over an especially pleasant thought.

We fantasized like that for hours and then leisurely walked back home in the late afternoon heat, rehashing some of the decisions we had made that day and half hoping tomorrow would be just as hot so we could do it all again.

If you have a close friend you care a lot about, why not do something special just for her? You could make a breakfast of eggs Benedict for just the two of you. Get rid of the hubbies and the kids. Get out the good dishes. Do it up right.

Or write her a thank you note for being your friend. Or knit her a scarf. Or send her a dozen balloons that say, "You're a great friend." Or clean her oven . . . that's if you *really* care for her.

Deep down friends like Lois are hard to find. If you have one, I'll bet you can think of something to do just for her that will make her extra happy this Christmas. After all, isn't that what friends are for? And isn't that what Christmas is for, too?

December 1986

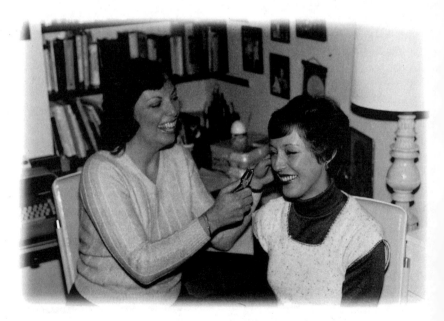

Who but a good pal lets you pierce her ear with a paper punch?

Random Thoughts

Little Sisters Sometimes Spy
Our youngest child, Annie, wanted to learn what her older brothers did when they sat on the screened-in porch with a girl. So she did what kid sisters (and brothers) have done for years: she spied! Then, equipped with precisely the evidence she sought, Annie rushed over to me while I made supper and tattle-taled, "They kissed, Mother! — lip to lip!"

Random Thoughts

The 90's Woman
My friend and co-worker Gayly stood in the doorway of my office watching me as I shuffled papers, talked to myself, poured a drop of coffee on my desk to remove a ring of milk at least two months old, and frantically stuck sticky notes on several new formed stacks of magazines on the floor around me. She looked amused but puzzled.

"I'm going out of town tomorrow," I explained, "and I want everything in order in case I get in an accident while I'm on this trip."

Gayly laughed and said, "Cleaning her office before a business trip is the working woman's version of making sure she doesn't have any rips in her underwear." Then she turned and left me to continue fulfilling this updated version of my mother's travel requirement.

Random Thoughts

Name Games
When I was a kid my parents called me "Li'l Ange" — short for "Little Angel." (You know how some parents are about their kids!) When my high school friends heard about that name, my bosom buddy Pat became known as "Li'l Dev" — short for, well, you get the picture — and those nicknames have stuck with Pat and me all these years.

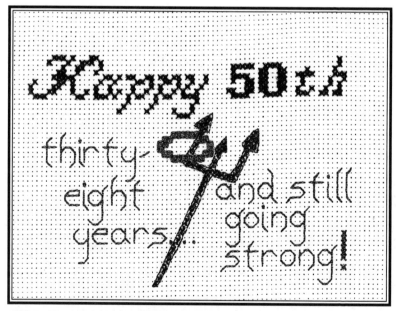

When Pat and I turned fifty, she gave me a marvelous cross-stitch piece. It celebrates our nicknames (the halo and pitchfork), our birthdays, and our friendship of almost forty years. Could she possibly have come up with a better gift?!!

My Teacher Is My Daughter

I'm a perpetual student. My education began over forty years ago with my parents as my first teachers. In all my life, they were the teachers who had the greatest impact on me. They taught me to dance, to look both ways, and to believe I was lovable.

During my formal education, my school teachers taught me to compute pi and bake pies, to construct sentences and algebraic formulas, to read French and computer printouts.

When I was a junior high teacher, I learned what every teacher learns: the kids teach you every bit as much as you teach them!

Now, even at this late date, I'm still learning. Today my most important teacher is my four-year-old daughter Annie. I have so very much to learn from her.

Annie reminds me that pretending refreshes. Five minutes of playing Toto to her Dorothy and the problems of my day seem far behind. Eating one of her imaginary dinners (served on invisible plates) has done wonders for my waistline. Being her daughter Veronica (she pronounces it Moronica) while she plays Mom gives me insights into my own parenting.

An evening of pretending with Annie, and I re-enter the real world feeling as if I've been on vacation in some resort paradise. I guess maybe I have.

More than once, this pip-squeak counselor has convinced me I'm not too old to daydream . . . to make believe . . . to stand with only one foot planted firmly in the ground. I'm still safe. I'm still responsible. I'm just a little younger after doing it.

My little professor has awakened me to the four-year-old girl who slept inside me . . . the one who likes tiny perfume bottles . . . who enjoys dressing and undressing dolls . . . who makes up songs that go on for five minutes with no rhyme and little reason

. . . who loves to snuggle and have her hair stroked and be told she's pretty.

That child in me still exists. I'm sorry to say she's often shoved aside by the busy adult who has taken over. But Annie brings back that little girl. I'm glad. I like that little girl. I've missed her.

Annie has brought me on a backwards journey I would never have scheduled on my own. But with her as my guide, I'm loving it.

So I've come full circle, I guess . . . from learning at home from my parents to learning at home from the last of my children. My parents taught me things I needed to know to get through life. Annie teaches me things I once knew but have forgotten. But oh! How I relish these lessons!

I enjoy learning – especially from outstanding teachers like my own kids. Who knows? With their tutelage, some day I may even earn a degree in All Grown Up.

September 1989

Snapshot from a Childhood

Let me show you a picture from 1956 which I always carry . . .

I sit at the kitchen table doing homework. It's late afternoon. The window is open; the white curtains blow gently. My mother is washing the dishes she used for preparing our dinner. She is singing — singing as naturally, as openly, as a bird.

She sets the last dish in the drainer and, still singing, hurries out to the yard. Rushing down the back stairs, she calls out a greeting to the old man sitting on the back porch next door. Although her step is fast, her voice carries no hint of impatience. As she takes down the sun-dried clothes, her eyes are on the neighbor, her words cheerful, and her inquiries about his health sincere.

When he has finished answering, she begins her song again. It's not a fancy song. Just a pretty melody with words that fit. Her voice is clear and easy to listen to. Her pitch is true.

She lifts the full laundry basket with an enthusiasm some reserve for only special events. Then she bounces up the stairs, calling a parting message to the neighbor. This time he grins and waves at her like a little boy.

She sets the laundry on an empty kitchen chair. As she picks up a dish towel from the top of the basket, she passes behind me, giving my shoulder a squeeze.

"Daddy will be home soon, honey. Time to set the table," she says as she slowly, almost dreamily, begins to dry the dishes with the still-warm towel.

As I clear away my schoolbooks, I look at my mom. Carefully, gently, she dries out mismatched dishes – as if they were the finest china and crystal ever made. There's a slight smile on her face. And I know that very soon my mother will begin singing again.

I recall that afternoon as if it were yesterday. I think of it often. But I wonder: Will my kids carry as loving a picture of me? I hope so. I truly hope so.

March 1987

Random Thoughts

A Trace of Sentiment
Mary Ellen, a colleague here at work, gave her mother a framed poem for Mother's Day. A few days later she received a tracing of her mother's hand and a note from her saying, "Not since I received one of these from you many years ago, have I been so touched by a Mother's Day gift." Now that's what I call a sweet thank-you note.

Spirit of Halloweens Past

When I was a kid, I always made my Halloween costume from things around the house. For whatever reason, I never had a store-bought costume. My mom and I would work it out together by going through her clothes closet, the linen drawer, and a box of miscellaneous accessories she kept for just such creative adventures. We would look through the stuff and, sure enough, something would trigger an idea.

Once we had determined what character I was going to be, we'd pull together the elements of the costume from that box of weird and wonderful odds and ends, tablecloths and runners, and the clothing of anyone living in our apartment . . . which at various times in my childhood included not only my parents but also my grandma, an uncle fresh home from World War II, and a down-on-his-luck family friend.

Then my mother would bring out her jewelry box. She would show me each piece, one at a time. Almost every bauble had a story to it. The spinning-carousel earrings her brother Howie had won for her at a shooting game in Riverview Park. The blue-stoned ring her Aunt Ollie had given her years before when the two of them had seen the movie "Phantom of the Opera" and my mom had stayed up all night crying. The brown shell necklace my dad had brought back from the Philippines — she wore it his first night home.

As she told me each story, I would try on the piece of jewelry. My favorite stories I would try on twice.

We would spend the entire evening of October 30th getting my costume together — the clothes and the jewelry. But on Halloween itself came the incredible experience of wearing make-up . . . with permission! My mother would set a chair in front of the bedroom mirror, so I could watch my own transformation.

At my request, the application included every tube, every pencil, every cream, every powder, every color, every vial — every possibility in her make-up drawer. Lipstick upon lipstick, rouge over rouge. Excess was impossible. Too much was not enough for me. And my mother went along with it.

Finally I was ready. I would leave my mom and pick up my friend Lois, also wearing a home-grown costume, and off we would go to gather the loot.

Lois and I would walk miles trick-or-treating. Then, as the afternoon wore on, we would pick up the pace and *run* from house to house, lifting a velvet hem to allow greater speed, removing a white glove to facilitate stuffing a Three Musketeers into a goodie bag. Near exhaustion, we would return home just as dusk turned to darkness.

As I look back on my childhood Halloweens, I can't single out a particular treat anyone gave me. There's just a blur of candy bars and cookies and apples in my mind's eye. Even the costumes themselves have become an avalanche of lace doilies, cut-up neckties, peasant blouses, and strands of necklaces.

But I remember to this day how wonderful it was to think up those costumes . . . just my mom and me . . . sitting on her bed . . . talking and making-believe together . . . laughing . . . trying on hats and scarves . . . examining lipstick shades . . . pretending.

October 1991

Second Mother

My mother died almost six years ago. I still miss her. But as time passed, I found myself turning more and more to my Aunt Elaine for the encouragement and support I missed from my mom. Even though I was well into my forties, I still needed a mother.

I'm not surprised I looked to my aunt for motherly love. She was a very warm person who had never had any children herself, but we had been close since 1962 when I stayed with her in California before my junior year in college.

That summer, Aunt Elaine taught me to sew. She was a real pain about it, too! If she made me rip out one seam, she made me rip out a hundred . . . until it was done correctly. I spent three weeks making and remaking the bodice of one dress! By the time I returned to Chicago, I had more than a great-looking dress — I had a new sense of who I was and what I could accomplish when I set my mind to it.

In 1978, Aunt Elaine and I vacationed in Europe together. My friends wondered why I traveled with my aunt, then the age I am now. "Because she's great company," I would answer with perfect honesty. Despite her appearance — dignified, proper, impeccably dressed down to the last detail — Elaine was a world-class giggler who found much of life enormously amusing. She could laugh at herself more easily than anyone else I've ever known.

On that trip to Europe, we visited Paris. It was wonderful! In addition to enjoying every moment of the city, I had a chance to practice the French I had learned back in college.

After listening to me for several days, Aunt Elaine decided she was ready to *parlez* a little *fracaise* herself. Dressed to the nines as always, she walked up to a sales clerk in a ritzy store and spoke to her in French. Although I couldn't hear what she had said, I was amazed because after a second's pause the clerk pointed her to the spot my aunt apparently wanted.

"So what did you say to the clerk?" I asked later as we walked.

"I said, 'Je suis un toilet,'" Aunt Elaine replied. "After listening to you I figured out how to say, 'Where is the bathroom?'"

I couldn't help but smile. "No, my dear aunt, you just told that sales clerk, 'I am a toilet.'" Elaine laughed until tears ran down her face.

For years, whenever she felt I needed to loosen up, she would whisper to me, "Je suis un toilet." She would get me every time.

My Aunt Elaine died this year. Going through her things, I found a box of audio tapes. I'd made for her – tapes of simple, everyday moments of my life from years ago.

Listening to those tapes was strange. I had forgotten virtually every taped conversation. There was not a single extraordinary exchange in the bunch of them.

But don't think for a second those weren't wonderful moments. I listened to my two youngest sons taking a bath together back in 1982. I heard our older kids, now in their twenties, as young teens playing Monopoly at the dining room table. I eavesdropped as my girlfriends and I watched the Bobby Riggs/Billie Jean King match on television in September of 1973.

On many of the tapes, I heard my mother. Sometimes she was telling me her grandchildren were surely the brightest and cleverest in all the world. Other times she was scolding my dad for teasing too much. Often she was in the background, singing. She sounded healthy and strong, happy and complete — just the way I love to remember her.

Those tapes of my mother, my children, and my friends were the finest legacy my Aunt Elaine could have given me. I have listened to them often and will cherish them always.

Sometimes after an especially trying day, I'll come home and put one in the tape player as I prepare dinner. I think about my mother and about my aunt. And I wonder who will next fill the role of second mother for me. Maybe my wonderful Aunt Mary. Or one of my daughters or sons. Or my husband Lyle. Or a good friend. But I know there will be another.

You see, I know from experience, when you need a mother, God sends you one. All you have to do is recognize her for what she is . . . and accept her gift of love as graciously as she offers it.

May 1994

The Other Half

The Case of the Disappearing Necktie

Sometimes — when I least expect it — I come face to face with the reason I love my husband. On a recent motor trip to a friend's party, I did just that.

Lyle and I had allowed three hours to drive from Chicago to Peoria for Barb and Mike's anniversary celebration — leaving ample time to check into the hotel and get dressed. But heavy traffic, a wrong turn, and a detour put us an hour behind schedule. Then Lyle had a brilliant idea.

"If you're up for an adventure, we can still make it on time," he said, with a glint in his eye. "How would you feel about changing clothes in the car?" I couldn't help but laugh. Then I realized he was serious! "We have all our stuff in the back seat, and we won't even have to stop except to change drivers. What do you say?" he challenged.

If I said no I knew I'd never live down being a party-pooper — and I really didn't want to miss any of the party — so I agreed.

Have you ever gotten undressed and dressed in a moving car? Have you done it since you've been allowed to vote? Since you've been married? Since you've had flabby thighs? It's not easy! There's virtually no room to maneuver, and you have to plan your every move. Plus it's incredibly silly, so you find yourself — or at least I found myself — laughing so hard you can hardly think.

But somehow or other, after about fifteen minutes I was dressed in my party dress and (the greatest of challenges) pantyhose. Lyle pulled off the road, he slipped into the passenger seat, I ran around to the driver's side, and we were off once again.

My difficulties were nothing compared to Lyle's! He weighs 200 pounds and is six feet tall . . . four feet of which are his long, long legs! He tore off his Bermudas, sandals, and T-shirt and threw them in the back seat. Arms and legs were going in all directions. It took forever! At last he sat catching his breath, stripped down to his boxers — blue with little red hats — while a backdrop of Illinois farmland played out behind him.

He brought his party clothes to the front seat and began dressing. He was able to pull up his trousers by putting all his weight on the balls of his feet and pressing his shoulders against the back of his car seat. He fumed and fussed and cussed as he struggled with his belt, shirt, and jacket. Even his socks and shoes weren't cooperative.

Just when I thought he had finished, he started looking around frantically. "Where's my necktie?" he snorted half under his breath. "I saw it when I got my things from the back seat." Lyle wildly searched under the seat and under himself, then frisked the clothes he had tossed into the back seat.

"A silk necktie can't just disappear while you're driving along at fifty-five miles an hour with the windows closed!" he sputtered.

We drove along in silence. Finally I offered, "If wearing a tie is that important, take off your clothes and search every piece." Reluctantly, Lyle agreed.

After several amazing twists and turns, he was, once again, half naked, riding along in only his boxer shorts. He diligently examined every stitch of clothing he had removed. No sign of the tie. Nowhere. No how. All hope now shattered, Lyle stared out the window. Stumped.

Then, in one last, desperate act, he stretched out the elastic waist of his boxer shorts and took one quick peek inside.

And at that moment, I was overwhelmed with profound insight: I love the little boy in Lyle. Yes, I usually see him as the wise and understanding father, the powerful and dignified businessman, the gentle and perceptive mate. But, oh, the innocent child in him really touches me.

Well, the tie wasn't inside his boxers, as you may have guessed. Lyle got dressed once more, resigned to partying tieless.

As we stepped out of the car at the party, something stuck out the bottom of Lyle's pant leg. "Look! My tie!" he squealed with the delight of a child recovering a favorite lost toy. "Static electricity plastered it against the inside of my pants!" He slinked it out, slipped it around his neck, and knotted it by the reflection of the car window. We ran into the party laughing.

A woman is truly lucky if beneath her husband's polished exterior — and silk necktie — beats the heart of a little boy.

February 1994

Our first year as a stepfamily, we each began to learn how to twist, turn, and bend.

A Stepchild's Firsts

Hard to believe the first of our six kids will be officially grown up next month. Scott graduates from college. Seems like only yesterday he was a little boy of fourteen. You see, as his stepmom, I didn't know him his first fourteen years. I missed out on his first tooth and first step. Still, I have enjoyed watching him grow up, and I cherish some very significant firsts he and I have had together.

I remember vividly the first time Scott and I worked side by side in the kitchen. We prepared a spaghetti dinner for the family. Scott was pretty comfortable cooking as long as everything was done exactly by the book (and I think he had read all of two).

He was aghast at the way I did many things, the often unorthodox but always practical techniques employed by many busy moms with large families. He couldn't understand why I wouldn't cut the onions, celery and green pepper into smaller pieces. Bigger pieces means less cutting and so it's faster, I said. When I threw the can of tomatoes into a large pot, he suggested I break them up with a potato masher. Too slow, I said, as I reached into the pot and with my bare hand squeezed each tomato into little pieces.

But when I put the package of ground beef into the microwave to thaw it, just the way the microwave instruction manual suggested, Scott could take no more. He rushed into the living room to report to Lyle.

"Dad," he said, hardly able to get the words out, "you know what she's doing *now*? She's *cooking* the meat before she *unwraps* it!"

I remember the first time Scott felt enough a part of our young yours-mine-and-ours household to help monitor the pets. Our cat Milky Way had a terrible habit of sitting on the stereo. Scott realized the cat could scratch the record if he decided to move while it was playing.

"Marie, what should I do with Milky Way to get him off the stereo?" he asked as a full participant in our new family.

"Oh, just throw him up in the air, Scott, please," I said, barely looking up from the book I was reading.

In seconds, one six-pound missile of screeching fur and claws went whizzing past me at fifty miles and hour! Scott had followed my instructions but he put his own spin on them. Instead of the gentle lope I gave Milky Way to get him back on the ground, Scott *threw* him into the next room — or maybe the next county — with all the muscle of a sixteen-year-old boy.

I remember the first time Scott told me he loved me — well, *sort* of told me he loved me. He and I had just had a disagreement, and I felt it was crucial that he know I still loved him even though I didn't like what he had done. I reached over, squeezed his hand, and said, "You know I still love you, Scott."

He risked it all when he whispered, "Me you too." Not the words traditionally strung together to convey fond affection, but no stepmother has ever heard three sweeter.

Now, in just one month, Scott begins a job in a town three-hundred miles from ours. So the last time he came home was truly the last time he came *home*. Next time he will be a visitor. As for his new firsts — first career paycheck, first apartment, first professional friendship — I'll miss being there for Scott's new experiences. And I'll miss Scott.

After all, this is a first for me: sending a child I love off into the world to seek his fame and fortune. It's a big step — even for a stepmother.

June 1987

My Dad, Bedtime Story Teller

I grew up in a four-room apartment on Addison Street in Chicago. The street was busy enough to need stoplights but quiet enough to nurture trees.

The room where I slept faced the street, and in the summertime the sounds of the evening drifted through its open window.

I lay there in my seersucker pajamas and listened. Car motors and brakes and occasionally a horn. Couples laughing during their evening walk. The baby next door crying for her last bottle. Radio music from a passing car, the natural song of a cricket. Wooden screen doors creaking open and slamming shut.

I watched the shadows in the room deepen as twilight turned to night. I followed the headlights from passing cars as they filtered through the trees and danced around the room. I turned my pillow over and over, searching for a cool patch.

And I waited. Waited for my dad to come in and tell me a bedtime story, a story made up on the spot, for me alone.

My dad wove wonderful yarns . . . gentle, slow-moving. There was never an interplanetary battle or a ring of spies on a dangerous world-wide mission. His were stories of people encountering everyday miracles, tales brimming over with minuscule details and observations . . . and oh how I loved them!

I remember one about a little girl four-years-old — probably my age at the time — who was given a beautiful orange. In exquisite detail my dad told about her peeling it, stripping off the white strings, separating it into segments, picking out each seed, arranging the seeds to form her initial, and ultimately enjoying every sweet, juicy bite of the fruit.

When the stories ended and my dad left me alone once more, I feel asleep — amidst the inconstant lights and intermittent sounds of that Addison Street apartment — feeling that my world was a fine, fine place.

That's my first memory of my father and I couldn't have asked for a better one. Memory or dad.

June 1986

Big Foot Lives

The morning I decided to wake up Jeff myself, I was the one who got the *real* wake-up call.

Since he was about ten — for maybe five years now — Jeff has been setting his alarm clock and getting himself up. But this particular day, I passed his room at six twenty-seven and decided I would awaken him for a change.

Having a few minutes to kill, I sat on the lower bunk — empty since our next son up the ladder had joined the Army and Jeff had promoted himself to upper-bunk status — and looked around the room. The wooden "Jeffrey" letters I had bought when Jeff was born. His E.T. doll and favorite stuffed toy Swannie, a white swan. On the top shelf in his bookcase, a stack of Syd Hoff books (including Jeff's beloved *Danny and the Dinosaur*) and his catcher's mitt.

The grandfather clock downstairs chimed only once before Jeff's radio began. Above my head in the upper bunk, I heard stirring. My little boy is waking up, I thought. "Good morning, Honey," I said. "Mommy came to wake you up today." A slow, deep grunt was the response. A grunt far deeper than I had expected.

For several minutes, Jeff tossed and turned and heaved and snorted like a big brown bear about to emerge from his cave after a winter's hibernation. Finally, propelled by one last, thunderous grunt, he sat up and threw his feet over the edge of the bed. Dangling inches in front of my eyes were his two feet — his two *enormous* feet!!

I gasped! Those monstrous feet were Jeff's? How had this happened? What had Jeff eaten for dinner last night?

Jeff paused at the edge of the upper bunk, still occasionally grunting, still mostly asleep. From the lower bunk, I stared at the two huge feet — and very hairy legs! — hanging before me! Jeff pounced to the floor and landed solidly on both of those feet. He plodded across his room— one big foot after the other — over to his robe hanging on the closet doorknob. Then he straightened up, stretched out fully — almost touching the ceiling — , slipped into his robe and lumbered off to the bathroom.

I sat there dumbfounded. Surely it was just a day or two ago when Jeff had little boy's feet. And only months before that, baby's feet — sweet smelling as baby powder, kissable, perfect this-little-piggy material. Overnight, he had dived into manhood — feet first.

Again I looked around Jeff's room. I now saw his computer. His planner with notes and reminders for himself. The program from Homecoming dance. His swim team towel. Salinger's *Catcher in the Rye*, Michael Jordan's *Rare Air*, Crichten's *Congo*. College brochures. A Duke Ellington poster, a trombone mouthpiece, a music stand.

Minutes later, Jeff came back in the room, now fully awake. "Jeff, honey," I said sympathetically. "Your feet . . ."

He looked down at them. "Yep, I think they're gonna be kinda big," he said. He wiggled his toes. Then he looked up at me and grinned through his braces — the same ear-to-ear smile he'd always smiled.

And I knew that same little boy was still there — there was just a lot more to him.

April 1996

Isn't It Romantic?

Romance is in the air these days, and it's not just because Valentine's Day is coming up. What's the hottest style in home decorating? Romantic, romantic Victorian with lots of lace, hearts, potpourri, and flowers.

Which movies are breaking records at the box offices? Romantic ones like *When Harry Met Sally*. And the older couples interspersed between scenes let us know it's okay to be romantic even if you've already cut all your permanent teeth!

What's happening to popular music? More romance! Now I hear Linda Ronstadt's voice drifting from my kids' rooms, and I wonder if it's really our daughter Susan listening to "It's Been A Long, Long Time". . . or if my father is manning Susan's stereo controls!

Oh, I'm not beyond being carried away by a romantic gesture. But I think the Scarlett O'Haras of the world and I look at romance very differently.

To me, romantic is a glass of freshly squeezed orange juice delivered bedside. Lyle often does that. (And when he does, he shows no sign of knowing that my flannel nightgown is missing half a collar. In turn, I don't care in the least that two of the three hairs which remain on his head are mussed up.) Simply, he knows I love o.j. in bed and he's prepared to make the necessary personal sacrifices to bring me that little pleasure. And I unconditionally accept his sweet gift.

Romantic is taking care of a sick child together in the middle of the night. Having been married for ten years now and having shared in the raising of our six children, Lyle and I have had many such romantic interludes.

Like the time early in our marriage when my son Eddie, then about six, had the flu. In the middle of the night, Eddie woke up crying, sick both north and south. The task at hand required both Lyle and me, and for two hours we tended to Ed. When Eddie finally fell into a healing sleep, I remember thinking how close I felt to Lyle. Even in my exhausted state, I knew my husband was "a catch."

Romantic is installing acrylic panels and weatherproofing strips in a screened-in porch together. There's nothing like it. We did that this fall. We sang songs while we worked. We started with a medley of Flying W country songs and ended with a few selections from Handel's *Messiah* . . . in two part harmony. We took a banana and eggnog break halfway through. Then after the kids had been tucked in, we put on our winter jackets and sat on the porch, praising ourselves for our hard work and ingenious job. The day was one of the most romantic I have ever experienced.

To me, romantic is holding hands in church . . . doing the Sunday Tribune crossword together in bed . . . pinching Lyle's bottom while he talks on the phone to the accountant . . . finding a note from him on my desk reminding me to make an appointment for my annual physical . . . discovering that he has given me the unbruised half of the pear.

And mostly it's being aware that I am lucky enough to have met and married a man who loves me in spite of myself. A man who is as imperfect and unique as I am. A man who has become the very best friend of my whole life.

February 1990

There Is Nothing Like a Name — Nothing in the World

The way I see it there are only three ways a nickname is born:

1.) Nicknamer finds nicknamee's personality so delightful that he simply must immortalize it through a cute and charming name.

2.) Nicknamer has such great admiration for nicknamee that he can't resist creatively reworking her given name into a clever moniker.

3.) Nicknamer is nicknamee's brother and knows the right nickname is the most direct route to sisterly insanity.

One night at dinner our daughter Lainie mentioned she disliked her middle name, Myrtice. The very next day at breakfast, her brothers said, "Pass the cereal, 'Myrtice.'" By evening they introduced her to their friends as "our sister 'Myrt.'" And by the weekend whenever Lainie walked through a room the boys would chant, "Myrt . . . Myrt . . . Myrt . . . Myrt" like a drum beat underscoring each of her footfalls. Inevitably Lainie would wail in frustration and bop one (or more) of the boys.

Then Lainie came up with an idea: She changed the pronunciation of Myrtice to Mer-TEECE. She thought it sounded glamorous and dignified — and it might stop her brothers!

Not a chance. The boys simply changed their chorus from the gutturally erupted, "Myrt!" to an airily whispered, "Mer-TEEEEECE." At all hours of the day or night, from out of nowhere you would hear, "Mer-TEEEEEECE! Oh, Mer-TEEEEEECE!" wafting through the house as if Heathcliff himself were calling.

How the boys delighted when they tormented Lainie
about her middle name!

The nightmare continued until Lainie finally followed my advice and laughed it off. Then the fun was gone for the boys, and they moved on to other challenges . . . like their sister Susan.

During a family holiday to Hawaii, our boys christened Susan with the nickname which remains hers to this day. Please recognize that they could have tagged her with any of a dozen different names suggested by various happenings of that vacation. But like Geiger counters heading straight for the mother lode, instinctively they went directly for the one name they sensed would incense her for years: "Snorkel Sue." Bull's-eye! By merely saying those words, they could reduce Susan to tears in under 37 seconds.

Without really trying to, our youngest daughter, Annie, outfoxed her brothers. She loved certain stories so much that she often took the names of her favorite characters. One day she'd call herself "Cinderella," the next day "Dorothy," then "Ariel." A new neighbor once asked me, "If it's not too personal, why did you name your youngest daughter 'Scarlett?'"

Because Annie kept changing the game, Scott, Ed, and Jeff could never quite put their hands around the material they had to work with. They never knew from day to day what name they were supposed to nick. They were, in no short time, at her mercy.

And after what Lainie and Susan have endured, I must confess I find it sweet indeed to hear Annie fondly call her brothers "ClapMan," "Eduardo," and "Jeff the Chef" . . . while the three of them are stumped for any name for her other than "Annie."

September 1994

EveryDay Matters

*Determination.
Eddie practiced it
before he knew
what it meant.*

Eddie Wins a Bibbo

I once lived on a small lake which held a Winter Carnival every February. The carnival was a wonderland of tastes, sights and sounds. Warm apple cider with cinnamon stick stirrers, plump hot dogs in poppy seed buns, and giant chocolate chip cookies. Big Band music on the p. a., outbursts of hearty laughter, skate blades scraping to a sudden stop, and the muffled applause of mittened hands appreciating an outstanding pratfall. Red woolen scarves, furry earmuffs, babies blanketed inside sleds and strollers, and steam from conversation and cigars and hot coffee.

And the Winter Carnival was skating contests. Exciting races for every age — over sixty to under five — with satin prize-ribbons so glorious even we grown-up skaters sharpened our blades the eve of the carnival.

My children and I had a tough time the first winter after their dad and I divorced. Their dad was still highly involved in their lives and he and I were kind to each other. But our family was now different from the other families on the lake . . . and the Winter Carnival was a *family* event.

Christmas, which fell six months after the divorce, was especially trying for Eddie, just three. But Santa had brought Eddie his first skates — a pair of double-blades he loved so much I half-expected him to sleep with them, and he was excited about skating at the Winter Carnival.

Eddie fell in love with the satin prize-ribbons almost before his skates touched the ice that day. "Eddie bibbo, Mama," he baby-talked, inspecting the ribbons up-close. I explained that he'd have to win a race to get a ribbon. He thought a moment, then reasserted, "Eddie bibbo," his brown eyes very serious.

Each time the loud speaker announced another contest, Eddie tugged at my sleeve, asking, "Now, Mama?" until finally it was the youngest skaters' turn.

There were few pre-schoolers racing that year. Two, in fact. Eddie and a four year old with a year of skating lessons under his snow pants. "Oh, dear," I said from the finish line, looking at Eddie thirty yards away. The starting gun sounded. The race was on!

The other skater sped across the ice, crossed the finish line, and pinned his ribbon on his jacket. Now all eyes turned to Eddie, still standing at the starting line.

Eddie took a breath, tucked in his chin, and began walking. You could never call what he did on the ice *skating*. Walking was the only thing possible in those double-blades. He walked — slowly, one abrupt step at a time — toward the finish line.

Our next-door neighbor cupped his hands around his mouth and called, "Go, Eddie." Almost at once the rest of us chimed in, "Go, Eddie . . . Go . . . Go."

That's just what Eddie did. He kept going . . . and walked the entire race. It took a very long time. When he crossed the finish line, the crowd went wild. They cheered and laughed. They smacked each other on the back. Somebody threw his hat into the air and whooped.

Eddie beamed, his prize-ribbon clutched in his little hand.

I skated to him, stooped down, and gave him a really big hug. "I am so proud of you, Edward! You didn't give up! You won!"

He studied his prize. "Eddie bibbo," he said solemnly. Then, starting at the left corner of his mouth, a tiny smile broke through and grew until Eddie radiated like an Olympic gold medal winner during the national anthem.

Second-place in a two-man race. Not much of a victory, you might say — unless you happened to be one of the lucky ones who saw Eddie's face as he crossed the finish line. We all knew Eddie was truly a winner. And the best part of all? Eddie knew it, too.

November 1995

Random Thoughts

Wild Women

When Eddie was in second grade, Laura and Sarah were both contenders for his deepest affection. One fall evening Eddie and I took a walk around the block, and he opened his seven-year-old heart to me.

"I like Laura, Mom, but she's wild. She's like a horse. A wild horse." We walked on as I patiently waited to see if he had more to say. He did.

"But Sarah is a quiet girl. A gentle girl . . .," then he held up his thumb and index finger in a sort of pinch, ". . . with about one inch of wild."

I instantly understood and knew Sarah would be Ed's chosen one . . . for the time being at least.

Oh, Brother!

Last week somebody accidentally belched during a meeting I was attending. The burper — a woman we all knew and liked — giggled one tiny giggle, apologized, and returned matter-of-factly to delivering her report.

Now there's a woman totally comfortable with the digestive system, I thought. She must have a brother.

Burps go with brothers like onions with chili dogs. Once our six kids — then ranging in age from Annie 3 to Scott 24—had stayed up until the wee hours playing board games and laughing. The next morning our teenage daughters met me in the kitchen before the others were up.

"Mother," Lainie said, her eyes flashing, "the boys have absolutely ruined Annie."

"Honey, I just checked on her, and she looked okay to me," I said returning to my morning paper and cup of coffee.

"Well, she's not okay. Not anymore!" wailed Susan. "Last night they taught Annie to belch! LOUD! And the worst part is she thinks it's funny!"

"No, Susan, the worst part is she's good at it!" Lainie continued. "Real good!"

Just then little Annie showed up in the doorway. She looked at Lainie and Susan, belched as loudly as a three-hundred pound man after Thanksgiving dinner, and continued on her way. Lainie threw her hands up in the air and squawked, "See, Mother!"

Upstairs the boys laughed. They thought Annie was simply wonderful. A really disgusting belch at such an early hour. Vulgar enough to upset both Lainie and Susan. What a gal that Annie promised to be!

Through the years, Annie has not disappointed her brothers. She continues to develop her skills by practicing often, I'm sorry to report. Recently some non-stop belching of hers brought me to the end of my patience. "Stop that immediately," I told her in no uncertain terms. Five minutes later Annie let out a really loud burp.

"Was that a *sincere* belch?" I asked heatedly. Annie stopped what she was doing and stared at me.

Although Annie has an excellent grasp of the language, she was stumped. "What's a *sincere* belch, Mom?" she asked wide-eyed.

"A *sincere* belch is . . . it's a . . . it's a belch that comes into being by its own power," I said, giving myself heartburn as I heard how pompous I sounded and saw how confused Annie still looked.

Although Scott has served as belch-guru in a pinch, Eddie is our resident expert and top innovator. Even now at age 22, he continues to refine (you should excuse the expression) and perfect his technique. Monday night as Ed headed out the door, he kissed Annie's cheek and, in one continuous sweep, belched into her ear. It resounded in the upstairs bathroom and bounced off the grandfather clock in the hall. Annie laughed so hard that Ed rewarded her with one more kiss.

Jeff, the youngest of our three sons, recently captured a live burp on his electronic keyboard. Then he transposed it into several different keys and tested it with different rhythms — a calypso burp, a jazz burp, and so on.

Finally, Jeff created and electronically recorded the song "Jingle Belch" — a musical tribute to tastelessness which will live forever in the annals of Clapper gastrointestinal history.

I used to believe raising boys was all baby powder and sweet hugs. Three boys later, I see it's much more down to earth. For some boys, the burp is the first step toward real communication. Boys belch and think that's funny so they laugh. Laughter removes defenses. With defenses gone, sharing thoughts feels less risky. They can then speak of events, ideas, dreams, even fears.

I'll confess: If it takes a belch to start a heart-to-heart with one of my boys — well, pass the diet root beer please.

(It's nice to know even a brotherless child like me can learn some of these finer points of raising sons.)

March 1995

Random Thoughts

What (on Earth!)'s My Line
When my son Eddie was little, he and most of his friends aspired to careers depicted on TV. Liam wanted to be an undercover agent. Jeremy wanted to be a private eye. Eddie outdid them both: He wanted to be "an undercover eye." Now that's really top secret!

Honeymoon Sweet

When Lyle and I got married, we didn't have a honeymoon. Oh, our kids did stay at Uncle Larry's on our wedding night. But the next morning the four of them were at our doorstep eager to link arms and begin our family journey six abreast.

Two years later, Lyle and I finally took flight on our honeymoon. Five glorious days in Albuquerque in a four-star hotel — in the Honeymoon Suite, no less! There was just one little glitch: our ten-month-old son Jeff accompanied us.

"In all my years at this desk, this is the first time anyone with a baby reserved our Honeymoon Suite," said the reservation clerk, making no attempt to conceal his shock as he checked us in.

"A honeymoon couple with the baby has a certain sweetness to it," said the bellman loading his cart with Lyle's suitcase and mine — and Jeff's suitcase and Jeff's diaper bag and Jeff's stroller and Jeff's back-carrier.

"Goo," said Jeff as the elevator took us to the top floor.

The Honeymoon Suite looked like a Hollywood movie set. There was a sunken tub in one corner of the room with a floor-to-ceiling mirror behind it. One enormous window revealed a breathtaking view of the mountains. The king-size bed had a gossamer canopy and silky curtains billowing all around. On the coffee table was an enormous bouquet of fresh flowers.

And smack in the middle of all this glamour? A crib.

The set may have resembled an MGM romance, but the action was straight out of Looney Tunes. A midnight tub-for-two loses its edge when your husband sits on a rubber ducky. A romantic fantasy is shattered when the romancers pause to pry open a ten-month-old mouth bent on snacking on a flower. And nothing

Although Lyle and I enjoyed our honeymoon, our pleasure paled miserably compared to Jeff's. He was fascinated by the wonders of the Honeymoon Suite —

the Jeff-sized waste basket —

the giant mirror —

and the best peek-a-boo bed a kid could dream of!

There's no denying it: Honeymoons are exhausting.

snuffs out the magic of an embrace in a gauzy four-poster like the inescapable aroma of eau de dirty diaper.

On our honeymoon, Lyle and I found ourselves half a world away from Paris, surrounded by baby bottles, a well-worn copy of *The Little Engine That Could*, and an ear-chewed Ernie doll. And in that setting, I saw a life that overflowed with the real things. I sensed that in spite of less than perfect conditions — which is all we've ever known! — Lyle and I would always enjoy each other.

On the flight home, I realized why Lyle and I will always be together. In time our *passion* will gently, slowly shift into *compassion* — but a romance founded on sweetness never really fades.

February 1996

An Important Gift from an Important Man

I've been given some wonderful gifts in my life. But one gift from my dad stands out above the rest as truly important.

As a lot of twenty-one-year-olds do, I had made some decisions my parents disagreed with. Although I had always had a close and loving relationship with them, they were hurt and somewhat angered by some of my choices. My mother, as soft-hearted and forgiving a person as there ever was, set aside our differences almost immediately. My dad was another story. Although we kept in contact, there was an awkwardness, a distance between us.

Late one afternoon, unannounced, my dad stopped by my apartment. He had brought me a present, he said, and handed me a package. When I removed the crisp, white paper, I found two big beautiful steaks inside. I looked at him, puzzled.

"They'll be good," he said. "They're porterhouses. The best the butcher had." I still didn't quite know what to make of all this. "Let's make dinner together," he said, and I knew everything was all right between us once again.

I never enjoyed a gift more.

Important gifts aren't given to reciprocate or impress. They are heartfelt, not rule-bound. They may be unexpected. They may be unorthodox. They may even be unappreciated.

Important gifts are important because they bring happiness. And they are given by people who care enough to send truly the very best: forgiveness, love, hope.

December 1987

Daddy on Demand

For a few hours last Sunday evening, my 12-year-old son Eddie and I switched places. He became the parent and I the child. Based on the way he treated me, I'll bet he's going to be a terrific Dad some day.

Eddie and I rode our bikes to a nearby high school to check out the tennis courts. Not being terribly adept at cycling, I took a curb in the school yard the way no one should ever take a curb. I was thrown from my bike and skidded across the concrete on my elbow.

When Eddie realized I wasn't behind him and I wasn't even on my bike anymore, he hurried to my side. His first reaction? Give Mom a hug. Pat her on the back. Kiss her cheek. Wipe away her tears.

Then he got a look at my injured arm. Immediately he was up and running.

"Eddie, where're you going?" I screamed, thinking this was no time for him to get even with me for insisting on a 10 o'clock bedtime.

"Internal bleeding," he shouted, still running. "I'm going for help!"

After I convinced Ed that this was *external* bleeding, the task at hand was to stop the bleeding and cover the wound so I could get home. Eddie promptly sat down and in a flash removed his shoes and socks. Before I knew what was happening, he had tied his socks around my elbow. The fact that these socks had probably been worn consecutively for three days gave me pause, but we had a solution.

Eddie assured me that when we got home, he'd properly dress the wound. "But first, Mom," he said tenderly, "we're going to have to scrub that with Lysol."

Lysol? The thought of it made me shiver. "We'll disinfect my elbow, but I'd rather use something a bit gentler than Lysol if that's okay with you, Doc," I winced.

On the ride home, Eddie watched me as a parent watches a toddler just learning to walk. If I fell behind, he automatically slowed down. When we neared a curb, he alerted me of the danger. At traffic intersections, he talked me through the correct way to cross a street on a bicycle. And we made it home just fine. Once there, he removed his socks from my elbow and gave me an official bandage.

Even though Eddie still has some of the first aid facts a little twisted, he certainly has learned how to properly administer tender, loving care.

Now I remember how bad it feels to skin your elbow . . . and how good it feels to have a Daddy who makes it all better. And if that Daddy is your own 12-year-old son, skinning your elbow can be a wonderful experience!

September 1984

A Uniform Decision

My son Eddie has liked uniforms since he was two years old. Back then, he gathered things from around our house to create his very first uniform . . . which he wore almost every day during the spring and summer of 1975.

Eddie's field shoes were knee-high rain galoshes his big sister Lainie had outgrown. Well, on Lainie they were knee-highs. On little Eddie they were hip boots.

The jacket was a sky blue, quilted karate robe with an embroidered bunny over the heart and satin ribbons that tied across his tummy. But it was size 12 months . . . so Eddie resembled a Jackie Gleason character stuffed into a suit coat three sizes too small.

The hat was a model railroad tunnel which fit Eddie's head as if it had been custom made. His curly brown hair sprang out the tunnel doors and windows, making him look something like a Chia pet come to life. Whenever Eddie wore his uniform in public, the first question people asked was, "What's that thing on his head? It looks like a model railroad tunnel. (Appropriate pause.) So, why's he wearing that thing?"

Eddie just loved that uniform! Each morning, he put it on as soon as he swallowed his last Cheerio®. Except for the hottest days, he wore that outfit until his bedtime bath. Sometimes in the middle of the night, he would climb out of his crib and put on the tunnel hat — the way some kids need a special blanket or teddy to help them sleep.

A few months ago, Eddie enlisted in the Army. For the next two years, he's back to wearing a uniform every day — but one very different from his first. All his curly locks are shorn and there's not a tunnel hat or an embroidered bunny in sight. Ed's still up in the middle of the night — 4:30 A.M. to be exact —

Ed and Jeff have a complicated relationship. Sometimes they play like two boys Jeff's age. Sometimes they play like two boys Ed's age. And sometimes they relate like father and son — with either of them assuming either role, depending on their moods.

putting on his uniform, but this time there's no snuggling under the covers for a few more winks.

Do I wish I could have chosen the uniform for this stage in Ed's life? Maybe had him join the Peace Corps? Or enlist for five years to qualify for more Army benefits? Or be a college student a few more years? Not my decision. And if there's one thing I've learned about my children, it is that their ideas and decisions are not necessarily uniform with mine.

This is Ed's life. He gets to call every shot. Because I believe Ed knows himself well, I have faith in his ability to make the right decisions for himself. And because I love him with all my heart, I support his decisions.

But I do wish one thing. I wish I could travel back seventeen years and tiptoe into that two-year-old's room. I would sit on the floor next to Eddie's crib, carefully remove the tunnel hat from his head, run my hand across those brown curls, and gently pat his bottom till he fell sound asleep . . . just once more.

August 1992

When I was pregnant with Jeff, following doctor's orders we took my two cats to live in our office temporarily. Lyle, a dog-person to the bone, declared, "It's okay under the circumstances, but I don't want those cats anywhere near me!" No one told the cats.

Our Recipe for Bacon

Lyle sat with his elbows on his knees. "I'm burned out, Marie," he said as earnestly as he'd ever said anything. Turning around our faltering business had taken him three years of relentless work and much self-sacrifice, but he had brought Clapper Publishing back to solid ground.

"I want to take a leave of absence," he said as he took both my hands in both of his. "I'll stay home and take charge of things here. Do you think you can manage the business without me for a while?"

"I'm certain it'll work out, honey," I said immediately. "Let's do it." Then we sat back, sipped our coffees, and dreamed what the next few months would be like.

Lyle pictured himself on a hammock surrounded by piles of books he had been dying to read. He was interrupted occasionally by one of our darling children who would plant a kiss on Dad's cheek and then quietly retreat into the garden to play amongst nature. Lyle was relaxed and fulfilled . . . in his dream.

I imagined myself dressed in a designer suit, walking very fast through a modern office building. Others hurried to catch up to me. Everyone asked me questions and sought my advice. I passed out directives as if they were breath mints. I was a woman comfortable with power . . . in my dream.

Then came the rude awakening.

During our role reversal, Lyle learned that nursing a child with measles is lonely and fattening. He learned that housewives pass many days without seeing any visible signs of appreciation. He learned there is no free time. He learned that mothering is as terrifying a profession as any other that deals with life and death.

He also learned that writing checks is as much fun as earning them . . . that working in a sweat suit instead of a three-piece is relaxing . . . that hearing a child say, "I love you , Mommy" (and that was what Jeff came to call Lyle) makes you warm all over.

I learned it's frightening to be a family's only breadwinner, the sole provider of milk and shoes and nights at the movies. I learned that "the buck stops here" leads to bouts of self-recrimination. I learned that business travel is always work, no matter how glamorous the setting.

I also learned that opening a lingerie drawer and finding clean undies someone else laundered and folded is delightful . . . that sitting down to a dinner you didn't prepare is sheer pleasure . . . that children look angelic when Daddy bathes and readies them for their bedtime story . . . that seeing one of your own concepts materialize into printed pages is thrilling.

After six months of switching places, Lyle and I eagerly returned to our previous lives. But neither of us wanted to go back completely. We had been to the other side of the mountain and knew its pleasure as well as its pain. So part of me remains the provider. Part of Lyle remains the caregiver.

That was 1983 — a year before "Mr. Mom" tickled every male and female funny bone in America. Looking back, I guess I'm glad we had the financial problems we did. Those troubles led us to try a lifestyle we would never have even considered. We discovered sides of ourselves which have made both our professional and our family life more richly colored.

Now Lyle and I both bring home the bacon. We cook it, eat it, and clean up afterwards — together. And we think it's delicious just that way!

May 1991

Random Thoughts

Dancing in the Dark . . . by the Light of the Silvery Coupe
Our family was tired and eager to get home after driving from Wisconsin. But just as we approached the railroad crossing, the warning bell sounded and the gate lowered. As the freight train began slowly chugging past, I sighed, settling down for a long, boring wait.

Out of the blue, Lyle asked, "Would you like to dance?" What a brilliant guy, I thought as I stepped out of the car into the middle of the road. He turned up the volume on the radio and joined me on the asphalt.

Of course, our kids — like, *totally* humiliated — begged us repeatedly to get back into the car. We danced anyway. Twirled and dipped until the caboose came along and the gates went up.

It was my favorite dance ever.

A Life in the Daze
of
One Woman

Banana Soup Wishes

I believe in wishing. On a clear night I still find that first star irresistible. To this day I wish on my birthday candles . . . although at my age I'm probably entitled to two or even three wishes per birthday.

When my pal Lois and I were kids, we weren't satisfied with one nightly star wish and one yearly birthday wish. We dreamed up excuses to make wishes. If, for example, a train passed, we raised both feet off the ground and wished. "Feet up! A train!" Lois would shout, and I'd lift and wish. We had dozens of trumped up wish-occasions like that.

The other night, for the first time in years, I invented a reason to wish. Annie, our six-year-old, began peeling a banana. Instead of making a clean start of it, she squeezed the top, the skin split, and squishy stuff squirted out the seam. By the look on her face, I knew Annie was about to reject the last piece of fresh fruit in the house. I thought, "I sure wish she'd eat that banana," and all of a sudden I had an idea.

"Annie," I said, "what a lucky girl you are! You've made banana soup!" I explained that banana soup is the magical stuff that squirts out when a banana doesn't want to be peeled. "Now you get to make a wish! Banana soup wishes are very rare and they almost always come true!"

Slowly Annie turned her head to look at me. Her eyes narrowed visibly, giving her an uncanny resemblance to my father thirty years ago when I came home from a school dance at two in the morning and told him the car had broken down. Annie locked eyes with me. Neither of us faltered.

"Banana-soup wishes don't come along every day," I added, busying myself by cleaning the kitchen counter, "and their magic doesn't last long. You'd better make your wish now and eat the banana," I said, smiling at her as I wiped.

She stared at the floor for a few minutes, thinking. Then she looked up with a big smile. "What should I wish for, Mommy?"

That brought us to the best part of wishing: deciding on the wish. We talked about all the possibilities, and finally Annie pinned down what she wanted. Then she worked on the wish wording, modifying it until the message was crystal clear. At last she made her wish, saying it out loud precisely as she'd refined it. She licked off the banana soup, gave me another big smile, and proceeded to eat the whole banana.

With every chew, her eyes twinkled as she pictured herself a famous ballerina, wearing a pink dress and twirling on a big stage . . . just as she had wished.

Perhaps Annie will be a ballerina someday. Wishing is very powerful . . . for grown-ups, too. What if we adults dreamed about the way we wished things were — in our families, on the job, in America? What if we pictured those wishes vividly and then turned our minds to that picture again and again and again — until the focus was so sharp it became reality? What if instead of wishful thinking, we tried wishful living?

Who knows? Maybe there really is a banana-soup fairy somewhere just waiting to hear from us.

February 1992

Joy Ride

I've never had a ride in a sleigh, one-horsed or otherwise, but I have had several memorable rides to and from Christmas celebrations. But one ride stands out above the rest: the Christmas Eve ride of 1946, the year my dad came home from the war.

I was four-years old, and that year my family celebrated its first holiday together in three years. We also celebrated our first car. Not a month after he was back home, my dad bought a '29 Chevy. It cost him $100 . . . and his watch.

Each Christmas Eve, my whole family gathered at Aunt Eva and Uncle Howard's. But that year, my dad, my mom, and I drove to their house in our car. No waiting on the corner for the Cicero Avenue streetcar for us! We felt like members of the upper crust, traveling in high style.

The evening was fun with food and gifts for the children as usual. But when it was time to go home, we had another wonderful treat: the ride back to our apartment . . . in the comfort of our very own automobile! Along the snow-covered Chicago streets, we chugged. Homeward bound — just the three of us — alone together in our cozy coupe.

The old Chevy smelled like musty dust and ashes. It was dark inside. The car creaked as we climbed in. I sat on my mom's lap in the front seat. I loved the clean smell of her skin, like lemon soap. She wrapped me in her well-worn fur coat to keep me warm. I felt like I was inside a magical cocoon. As I breathed in and out, the hairs from her coat tickled my nose just enough to keep me drifting in and out of sleep.

As we rode along, I listened to my parents' voices. They thought I was asleep. They spoke softly and briefly to each other. My dad's voice very deep, my mother's light and delicate. The air in the car was so cold their words seemed suspended just beyond their mouths. I wondered if I could reach up and snap them off, like icicle sentences.

Ten minutes later we were home. My dad parked the car on Addison Street, right in front of our apartment building. Then he came around to my mom's side and very gently, very surely lifted me out of the car. I was half asleep, half awake as he carried me upstairs to our first-floor flat.

I felt so happy. My daddy was home. I was warm and safe. And tomorrow was Christmas.

I will never have another Christmas ride quite like that one. Perhaps it stands out most because on that ride, on that night, I made a choice which has set the direction for much of my life: I chose hope.

Looking back, I realize I might have made a different choice. After all, my family had very little materially. My dad was not only out of a watch, he was also out of work. He and my mother were reestablishing their relationship after a three-year separation. It was trying for them both; each had changed so much during those years apart. And I didn't really know my father at all. I was an infant when he left; he was a stranger when he returned. But, in spite of all that, during that Christmas ride, I chose hope.

The important stuff of Christmas rides is never the vehicles we have or the destination we set out for or the distances we go. What's important is the way we see the journey itself. The journey to Christmas is always a miracle of hope waiting to happen for us. All we have to do is choose it.

This Christmas, you can still choose hope. If you do, you may find yourself on a joy ride that will last your whole life long.

November 1993

*My parents showed me countless examples of
how to recognize and savor a moment of joy.*

Christmas Spectacles

The first time I put on a pair of eyeglasses I was amazed! Flower colors were brighter than I'd ever before seen them. Trees were more defined. I saw things I'd never noticed — branches, leaves, and even buds! I could amuse myself for hours by simply putting on my glasses and looking around.

Just a few years ago I had a similar experience. My husband Lyle changed my viewpoint by doing something shocking: He shaved off the beard and mustache he had sported for a decade.

"What's wrong with your face?" I gasped, seeing him with a bare face for the first time in years and not figuring out what he had done. "Something weird has happened to your lip." All he could do was laugh. "Wait. It's your teeth! Your teeth are naked." Then I figured it out. "You've shaved! Why on earth did you do that?"

Lyle explained he wanted me to notice him the way I used to. He said I'd become so comfortable looking at him I seldom saw him any more.

Well, he had my attention, all right! In fact, I couldn't take my eyes off him! His face wasn't actually any different, of course, and he was certainly the same person. But his eyes seemed bluer and his smile fuller. He had cheeks and a chin . . . or two. I was fascinated.

One year my friend Aleene realized Christmas celebrations were becoming routine, so she hung her Christmas tree upside down from the ceiling! Her children and grandkids sat around for hours admiring the ornaments (the same ones Aleene had used for years) as if seeing each one for the first time.

I like the way those bold moves of Lyle and Aleene reawakened the beauty and value of the familiar. That has inspired me to give a new slant to one of my family's holiday traditions: Christmas dinner. I haven't decided exactly what I'll change, but I'm determined to shake things up a little this year.

Maybe I'll turn our usual buffet into a formal, sit-down affair. (That should rock the boat!) Or remove everyone's shoes as they enter the dining room and slide their feet into brand new, fuzzy slippers. Instead of asking Lyle to give the blessing I might ask everybody to stand, hold hands, and all sing grace together. Maybe I'll replace the venerable pecan pie with birthday cake, complete with dozens of candles!

But, oh, this year I want to take their breath away for just one moment . . . as if they all put on Magical Christmas Spectacles, spectacles which immediately bring into sharp focus the delightful surprises life has waiting around every corner. Perhaps this is the way God — with His perfect vision — always intended us to see our world: an uncommonly wondrous place brimming over with unlimited opportunities for joy . . . if we will simply open our eyes to the possibilities.

Look for the joy in your world this Christmas. It's there . . . just waiting to be seen.

November 1992

Let the Music Play

When I was in seventh grade, I started playing piano. Well, it wasn't actually piano I played; it was the Cardboard Keyboard. Every day before school, I'd drag out three octaves of cardboard, set up on the dining room table, and practice for about twenty minutes, singing my little heart out as I played. Then twice a week we Cardboard Keyboard students got to play the real piano in Mrs. Heinrick's room. Now that was a thrill!

I think my parents took pity on me (listening to someone practice "When It's Springtime in the Rockys" on a slat of cardboard is pretty pathetic) and decided to buy a piano. At a nearby tavern they found a forgotten, out of tune piano I thought was perfect (it made music) and so did they (only $25). My dad — with assistance from Uncle How and Uncle Al — moved the piano from The Mandarin Inn to our first floor flat as all the kids in the apartment building watched.

The piano was bright red with a multitude of cigarette and cigar burns, stains from spilled drinks and bottle bottoms, and chipped ivories. One look and you knew this piano had tasted life, even if it was the seamier side. But I loved it! I started lessons at a neighborhood music studio and learned at a very fast clip. By the end of my first year, I was asked to accompany the dancers during their rehearsals.

Then I turned thirteen. Hello, boys; good-bye, Schaum.

My formal musical education stopped but I still played . . . not every day, mind you, but often. Music continued to bring me pleasure and release.

Throughout my teens and later when I was going through a divorce, I would work myself out of a bad mood by banging out a song or two. What I lacked in quality, I made up for in volume . . . and I always felt better afterwards.

When my mother became so ill with Alzheimer's Disease that there was little in life which brought her pleasure, I realized she still liked hearing me play piano. So, when I visited her, I brought my book of popular music from the 30's and 40's. I played and she sang. Almost until the very end, even after she had lost the ability to construct a sentence, she would sing along, seldom missing a word.

This year for my birthday my husband Lyle gave me piano lessons. I was delighted but a little scared. It had been over thirty years since I had been a piano student. As life would have it, my five-year-old Annie had her first piano lesson ever on the same day as my reentry into the music world. Annie is in a class with three little friends she knows from Sunday School, and I am in what can only be called a class by myself. But both Annie and I are having a great time.

Even if you must start with a Cardboard Keyboard and graduate to a second-hand upright, make music . . . with a piano or a crochet hook or a garden hoe. You don't have to become a pro, and you don't even have to be the best you can be. Just enjoy it! Become absorbed in something outside yourself. Let it soothe you. Let it bring pleasure to others. Find that special music that lifts you above life's harshness . . . and play it with gusto all your life!

September 1991

Friends and family celebrated my dad's 76th birthday with a parade in his honor.

Before the Parade Passes By

At 9:30 a.m. on a sunny Saturday, all able-bodied members of our family met on a Chicago street, two blocks from my dad's house. We put the top down on my husband Lyle's convertible, poked flags into the window slots, and decorated the sides with banners that read, "Happy 76th, Chet."

All the while we were getting things ready, we could see my dad watering his front lawn. We were a rowdy group (as always), but my dad never did look over at us. He was busy sprinkling his lawn, waiting for Lyle and me to show up and take him for birthday pancakes as we'd planned.

My son Jeff had a trombone to play, but the rest of us chose toy instruments to herald our coming. We tuned our instruments (now THAT was a laugh), Ruthie practiced her baton twirling (an even BIGGER joke), and we lined up behind the convertible. With a loud wah-wah-wah-wah from the trombone, the parade began.

My dad told me later what went through his mind as our band of merrymakers marched toward his house:

"Must be some kids going to a ball game. I think they're coming right past my house. Why are they so loud? That's an unusual combination of people for a parade . . . That car looks just like Lyle's. Wait a . . . It IS Lyle's car! And Lyle's driving it! What's Lyle doing with all those . . . That's my grandson playing the trom . . . What's my nephew Don doing with . . . There's Al . . . Chrisy."

When my dad figured out what was happening, he broke out laughing. He laughed and pointed at us and laughed some more. Ultimately he pointed the watering hose straight up in the air so he was standing beneath a shower laughing, laughing.

We insisted my dad get into the car and sit up on the back like a celebrity. We drove around his block, and we waved to his neighbors, causing quite a sensation.

This idea began when my dad mentioned he was one of the last soldiers to return from World War II, and by that time all the parades were over. I figured he deserved a parade . . . as a Life Hero.

A parade is a great party, if I say so myself. There's very little planning or expense. You don't really need a convertible; in fact, you don't even need a car. You can probably rig up something just fine with a wagon. Kids' instruments are a real plus, but kazoos or tissue paper and combs will do.

So all you really need is a hero. I'll bet you know one. And if your hero is anything like my hero, you'll be bringing a lot of happiness into his life . . . and into your own.

September 1992

Don't View . . . Do

After Sunday's service, some junior high kids stood outside church planning that evening's youth-group activity. Kathryn, a really neat teenager, couldn't decide if she should come back for the party or stay home to watch the Bulls basketball game on television.

"Kathryn," I blurted out as I headed for my car, "in your whole life you won't have another chance at tonight's fun with your friends. Choose *doing* instead of *viewing*. When I do, I'm happier!"

For years, I've been aware that television depresses me. Then recently I read that I'm not alone in that feeling. When asked to rank various activities on the satisfaction and happiness they evoked, people stuck TV at the bottom of the list! Even cleaning closets got a better happiness score!

If TV is really so depressing, why do we spend so much time with remote controls in our hands, watching *My Little Margie* reruns and recipes for Creole carob cakes and the temperature in Zimbabwe? I think because television is addictive. It moves. It changes. It attracts us. First we get drawn in, then hypnotized, then ultimately addicted.

Years ago, I walked into our family room to find Eddie, my five-year-old son, intensely watching a Japanese movie with English subtitles! He couldn't yet read and he certainly couldn't understand Japanese, but he sure knew how to be mesmerized by motion, color, and sounds.

Please don't misunderstand. I think TV has its place. It's a great way to learn certain things — like how to make a French knot and what if feels like to walk through Buckingham Palace. It helps me control my weight: I find the stationary bike not nearly so unattractive if I can catch up on the day's news as I pedal. And after a hectic business trip, there's nothing more relaxing than vegging out in front of the tube in my jammies with a bowl of popcorn.

But television can become a habit that's very hard to break. Hundreds of people — all of them living alone — were offered a handsome sum of money to stop watching TV for one month. Over half quit mid-month and forfeited the reward because they simply couldn't stand it! They didn't like being *alone*, they said.

Television's especially alluring for people living alone because it feels like company. After all, it *is* voices and faces. More than once, I've found myself thinking of talk show guests as my friends. And unlike my in-the-flesh pals, TV personalities never lose patience with me, never pass gas in my presence, and never confront me. But those relationships aren't *real*.

And I'm all for participating in *real* life. Instead of passively watching plastic, perfect, predictable television, I think we're happier when we *do* — when we *do* almost anything! Telephone a relative. Write a note to a friend (don't worry about the spelling; she won't even notice). Take a walk. Make a craft. Read anything with pages (cereal boxes don't count). Pick out a song on the piano. Pick out the fleas from your dog's fur. Don't *watch* basketball; *play* basketball!

If you can't think of anything else to *do*, clean a closet. It is spring, you know. It does need doing, you know. And you just might discover that belt you borrowed from your cousin three summers ago and thought you'd lost. Or the first drawing your oldest child brought home from kindergarten. Or how wonderful you feel when you entertain yourself.

P.S. My son Jeff told me Kathryn showed up at the party that night. He said it looked like she had a pretty good time . . . and the Bulls did just fine without her.

April 1994

Listen . . . Care Fully

Jeff's gums throbbed and his head ached after wearing his new braces for four hours. Lyle and I tried to ease his discomfort — a chocolate shake, extra pillows for his head, two Tylenol and a foot rub — but nothing helped.

Annie did her part, too. "I'll sleep in your room tonight, Jeff, in the spare bunk," she volunteered, enjoying the role of a seven-year-old Florence Nightingale. "Then if you need anything I'll be right there for you." Jeff moaned softly. "And because you're such a great brother," she oozed, "I'll tell you a long, long bedtime story." Jeff moaned loudly.

Once they were settled in their bunks, the kids and I said prayers together — one in unison, followed by personal prayers from each of us. But no sooner had we said "Amen" than Annie indignantly snapped, "I heard an insult in that prayer."

Jeff and I were dumbfounded. An insult? I certainly hadn't been aware of one — and I would expect an insult nestled inside a prayer would be obvious!

"Jeff did insult me, Mother," insisted Annie. "I heard him say, 'Annie's my pain,' right in the middle of his prayer!"

Jeff laughed a little and said, "I didn't say, 'Annie's my pain.' I was thinking about my new braces and I prayed, 'And ease my pain.'" When I closed Jeff's bedroom door, he and Annie were still giggling as she began her bedtime story for him.

But I realized something strange about people: We listen funny. Because we're self-centered, we think all words lead to us. And because we know we're imperfect, we listen for rejection — even those of us who have been showered with love listen for it.

There are times I swear I "hear" Lyle say, "You don't know much, Marie," when he's really trying to impress me with *his* knowledge of computers.

I "hear" my friend Carole say, "You're weak, Marie," when in truth she's telling me *she's* happy to help me with a problem.

I "hear" my dad say, "You fall short as a Mother" when he means *he's* delighted to be useful as a parenting mentor.

I believe we all want to be good listeners, but we're wrapped up in ourselves. It's hard to set ourselves aside and receive messages from another person. Still, every time we do, relationships blossom. Life becomes a little less lonely.

An hour later, I checked on Jeff and Annie. I just stood outside the door and listened for a few minutes. I liked what I heard: Annie was still going strong with the bedtime story, putting high drama and intense emotion into each sentence . . . and Jeff was snoring.

February 1993

Christmas Album

I recently read the suggestion that once a year the family camera bug should take a roll of black and white shots of family members. Color photos, the experts find, fade in time. Black and whites, on the other hand, maintain their quality as the years pass.

That made me think of some black and white candids taken one Christmas Eve in the mid 1940's. My cousins Karen and Donny and I, three little kids playing in front of the Christmas tree.

There's one photo I particularly love. Karen wears a chenille bathrobe, and her hair is in pincurls. She's leaning over a little wooden ironing board, certainly a gift from Santa, elbows propped on the board, toy iron in one hand. Her eyes, enormous with delight, twinkle, and even though she's biting on her lower lip, she still can't hide her smile.

Wearing a pinafore, I sit on the floor, my legs straight out in front of me, one shoe on, one shoe gone. My hair is toussled, with a single barrette clinging to what remains of braids pinned atop my head. I'm wearing a little frown, and my cheeks and mouth are puffed out with air as I try to unbutton dolly's dress with my chubby fingers.

Donny is oblivious to the camera. Rapt, he studies the principles of physics as he spins a top. He wears slippers, pajamas, and a Hopalong Cassidy holster.

Behind us is the Christmas tree. The tree ornaments are barely distinguishable because the lights . . . the wonderful lights . . . are little pops of brilliance, softening everything else in contrast. They bathe us in hazy wonder. Our hair looks like gossamer. Our faces glow. There are unidentifiable shadows. There are silhouettes. The photograph is as mystical and wondrous as Christmas itself.

Black and white film does that. It grasps the drama of black, the electricity of white, the subtleties of gray. The eye is not seduced by color. The story is not diluted by reds and yellows. You are required to fill in the colors . . . from memory. And in the process, you relive the moment.

The real colors of Christmas are vibrant. Just the same, maybe you'll take some black and white snapshots this year. Then you'll have a record of the breadth and soul of this Christmas. You'll have prints of the illusions, the spirits, the veils of your celebration. And years from now, you will look at those images . . . and remember.

May you experience this Christmas in full color. May its memory stay with you forever in soft impressions of shadow and light.

December 1990

A Touchy Subject

I travel almost twenty miles to get a haircut. In the suburbs of Chicago, that's most unusual, because there are nice beauty shops on practically every corner. Still, I've gone to this shop for over ten years. Yes, the stylist who cuts my hair is wonderful and gets it to behave better than anyone before him ever did. But it's the shampoo girl that keeps me coming back.

The shampoo girl is a middle-aged woman. I know she works hard, and she knows the same is true of me. Over the years, we've talked about husbands, kids, and life — both the good times and the tough parts. We gab until she's ready to wash my hair; then we're both silent.

Her fingers massage my scalp firmly, but her touch is gentle. After the rinse, she takes out a wide-toothed, wooden comb. With her right hand she carefully works the comb through one section of my hair at a time. Then she runs her left hand across the newly combed strands, humming softly as she does. It's a slow process, and she doesn't hurry. Comb, smooth, comb, smooth, comb, smooth. So tender, so kind. By the time she's finished, I'm so relaxed that my worries seem a million miles away, and I feel like a new person.

Babies have it made. They get touched all the time. God made them so round and soft and shiny almost no one can resist hugging and cuddling them. I think that's why they thrive as they do; they're touched all the time and it makes them feel great! Sure they're growing teeth, they have wet bottoms, and they have a hard time expressing themselves. But they find comfort in life . . . and that comfort is in a touch.

During the last six months of my mother's life, she comprehended less and less. Near the end, I just sat next to her, holding her hand. I rubbed and patted her hand and her arm . . . and talked or sang softly to her. Touching was the last way I had to tell her I loved her. I know she understood.

The first summer of her life, Annie often took a Sunday nap on the porch glider with her daddy. Held by someone who loves her. Rocked gently. Embraced by love. What a beautiful way to fall asleep!

We humans need to be touched. There is such solace in it, such comfort. Oh, I'm not talking about the politician's touch or the seducer's. I'm talking soul to soul. Figuratively and literally, touching removes the barriers between people.

So the next time a friend tells you she's worried about losing her job, touch her arm as you give her encouragement. That may be just the extra strength she needs to get through the day.

If your son talks about a bully he has to deal with on the playground, guide him with words of courage and hope . . . and stroke his hair as you do. He'll carry the warmth and love of your touch with him for days, long after the words are forgotten.

When you meet your elderly neighbor on the street, put your arm around her as you walk together. There may be no one else in her life to touch her, and touching heals. Give her that boost. It will lighten her heart . . . and yours.

Touch. Skin to skin. About as simple as you can get. But the message a touch conveys is clear: Everything is going to be all right . . . I feel with you . . . You are not alone.

June 1993

Bad Manners Night

I'm so grateful there's an April Fool's Day — the one day we don't have to act serious, proper, or grown up. In other words, we can be our silly ol' selves!

Getting in touch with the silly little kid inside may not be easy, but I think it's worth the effort. Kids really are thrilled when an adult surprises them with the kind of behavior they expect only from a playmate. To a child, a little silliness can transform a grown-up into a real live person!

Why not take advantage of April Fool's Day? Do something silly with your kids. Like Bad Manners Night. Instead of insisting the kids use their *best* manners, insist they use their *worst* table manners . . . short of throwing food or taking someone else's food. (Lyle and I installed those rules three seconds into our first Bad Manners Night. Unfortunately, we were three seconds too late.)

Instead of plates, use lids or other wobbly stuff. Use bowls or pots in place of glasses. Silverware? Out of the question.

On our first Bad Manners Night, I explained the idea to the kids as I passed around the lids and pots. The older kids loved it and could hardly wait to start blowing bubbles in their milk. But Eddie, who was four, asked with a sob in his voice, "Where's my NAP-kin!" I knew he was going to have trouble coping. Over the years, however, Ed has made a remarkable adjustment to this April event. He has, in fact, been down right inspired at times.

Bad manners actually teaches kids about good manners. Gives them a sense of why we have etiquette in the first place.

Whether you try Bad Manners Night or prefer less of a commitment to silliness and simply show up for dinner wearing galoshes, a robe, and a tiara, this April Fool's Day get into silly. Silly leads to laughter. And laughter leads to happy. And what's so foolish about that!

April 1983

Random Thoughts — *good*

Collaring the Market on Silly

Recently I bought The Silencer Collar to help break Jazzabelle, our lovable Sheltie, of her perpetual barking. This high-tech device sets off an alarm whenever there's "nuisance barking." It doesn't hurt the pup at all but startles her in mid-bark so eventually she quits yipping so much.

Hopes were high Friday night when I first buckled the collar on Jazz. By noon Saturday, we had heard plenty of barking but no alarm and wondered if the collar worked.

Lyle — my husband, my hero, the father of six, and president of Clapper Communications — took the collar off Jazz, buckled it around his own neck, and barked loudly. The Silencer Collar remained silent. Meeting with no success, he passed the collar to Lainie, our twenty-four-year-old philosophy major. She gave it her all, I swear, with loud barks and colorful howls. The collar was mute. Then Susan put on the collar and barked, Eddie (home on leave from the Army) barked, Jeff barked, and Annie barked.

In a sea of silence (except for Jazz barking in the background), the defeated group headed for the nearest ice cream parlor to drown their sorrows.

Once alone, I looked at the collar. Too bad it didn't work, I thought. I turned it over and wondered if the volume was correctly adjusted. That's when I saw the compartment for the batteries . . which I'd forgotten to insert!

Great Un-Expectations

Sometimes life's unexpected curves delight us more than our best laid plans. Like the time heavy fog changed the plan of action I had designed for our daughter's graduation day.

I had planned every detail of our trip to Southwest State. My husband Lyle, our four youngest kids, and I would fly in our twin-engine plane to Marshall, Minnesota. Instead of a grueling ten-hour auto trip (which our family couldn't complete in less than sixteen), we would have a fun two-hour plane ride, share in Susan's big day, and be back home Saturday afternoon just twenty-four hours after we had left.

Mother Nature had other ideas. Around lunch time on Friday, a record-breaking fog rolled into Chicago. The weather bureau forecast no improvement for two days, so flying was out of the question. Lyle and I had no sensible choice but to drive — all 542 miles there, 542 miles back — with the six of us scrunched inside our sedan.

My mind raced as I formulated Minnesota Master Plan, Version Two. I phoned my daughter Lainie and told her, "We're not flying to Susan's graduation. Grab the bathing suits and be ready to leave in 15 minutes."

There was a long pause at the other end of the phone. Then Lainie asked incredulously, "We're _swimming_ to Minnesota?"

My new plan had a few holes. Yes, I had the foresight to call for bathing suits so we could swim (we would now be spending at least two nights at a hotel), but I had forgotten audio tapes, games, books, magazines, pillows, and snugly toys. In short, Lyle and I were unarmed.

By the time we reached the outskirts of town, I had exhausted my personal repertoire of car activities. Desperate, I began telling the kids about the book I had just finished reading which had an exciting, historical story line with colorful characters. To stretch it out over as many miles as possible, I included every little detail I could recall.

That was the first surprise of the trip: The children enjoyed listening to me tell them an intricate story — like I enjoyed a good radio story when I was a kid. If they had a question, I would simply put the story on hold and give a complete answer.

The kids could nod off if they felt the urge. They could interject a related incident from their real lives or their reading experiences. The darkness surrounding them made them feel especially comfortable saying whatever they felt. We could rewind, rerun, or fast forward the story as we wished. It felt almost as if time stood still as the miles sped by. The kids loved "listening to Mom's book."

Other out-of-the-ordinary things came our way because of our changed plans. Leisurely driving back after the graduation, we chanced upon the childhood home of Laura Ingalls Wilder, one of the girls' favorite authors. The kids begged to visit her farm and the tiny church on the homestead, and so we did. It was very charming! And because it wasn't part of a blueprint drawn up by Mom, the kids felt as if that side-trip to Walnut Grove was their special contribution to the weekend.

In Galena I was intrigued by some antique shops. As we stepped into the street after parking the car, we heard, "Hey! Clappers!" It was Brian, a good friend from New York City!

We all had breakfast together, and he was delighted to meet our kids, whom he had never before met. That chance meeting was especially important to Lyle and me because it was the last time we saw Brian. He died later that year. But we've always been grateful our kids had the chance to at least talk and laugh with him once.

Sunday night as we pulled into our garage, I realized what a great weekend we had had. Virtually nothing had gone according to my original plan — but the weekend turned out to be one of our family's most fun ever!

I had a good plan for our family the weekend of Susan's graduation. But looking back, there's no doubt that Mother Nature's plan was even better.

August 1994

Learner's Permit

Last fall, Lyle and I collected for the Lions' Club. We spent a Thursday evening and a Friday morning at a busy intersection near our home asking motorists if they'd like to contribute. In exchange for a few hours of my time, I learned a lot about one of my favorite subjects: people.

1. Some people are so busy their cars have become moving dining rooms.

The phrase Meals on Wheels has taken on a whole new meaning for me! I had no idea how many people eat in their cars! Now, granted, Lyle and I approached people at mealtime. Still, I was truly amazed! Drivers weren't simply popping a piece of candy or a grape into their mouths. At stoplights, they built sandwiches — with loaves of bread, peanut butter, and jelly jars balanced on the console in the front seat. As they shifted, they downed plates of fried eggs, bacon, sides of hash browns, and coffee — with napkins and salt and pepper shakers resting on the glove box. But the Too-Busy-To-Eat-Without-Moving Award goes to the family of six stuffed into their compact car — all eating sushi with chopsticks as merrily they rode along.

2. Some people live in fear.

More than one person locked her car door as I approached. Now, I can understand someone doing this with Lyle. Although he's very harmless looking, he's a big guy. But me? What did they think I was going to do in full daylight at a busy intersection? Jump in next to them and rip coins from their purses? Their actions, irrational as they were, are a sad but revealing commentary on our times.

3. There are those who refuse to let any tragedy, any burden, anything stop them.

A driver with no arms made a donation. He drove a special car which he maneuvered with his feet, and he seemed to be on his way to work. It took him a while to get out his money, but eventually it was added to the Lions' collection can. He said he was happy to help someone less fortunate than he was. I just smiled feebly, not trusting myself to speak.

4. Teenagers are remarkably giving.

Without exception, every teenager made a donation. I know sometimes they donated lunch money and certainly most of them didn't have a surplus of cash. But whatever they had, they shared. Not one of them even hesitated.

5. I still have a lot to learn about people.

Sometimes I get smug because I think I know people pretty darned well. I've always enjoyed others and I've paid attention to them during my fifty years, so I tend to think I have a solid understanding of what makes them tick. But this experience really opened my eyes. I have a long, long way to go before I'm a wise woman, believe me. A long way.

When our morning ended and Lyle and I turned in the donations we'd collected, I felt invigorated. I had looked into the eyes (and cars) of hundreds of people — people who were funny and charitable and friendly and rushed and frightened and eager and determined and, in short, some of God's best work.

September 1983

Through a Child's Eyes

Last Sunday, Annie and Jeff asked if we could skip church and instead worship at home. My "baloney detector" switched on. We'll plan everything, they said. A six- and an eleven-year-old planning a worship service? I had visions of half an hour of sacrilege — an excruciating thirty minutes of "Rub-a-dub-dub, thanks for the grub" sort of stuff.

But an hour later, Lyle and I sat down in the living room, still not knowing what to expect. Annie opened the service by reading from the Bible — not King James or American Standard but a Children's Bible of Jeff's. She had chosen the Story of Creation as her first reading. Only once did she say, "Now let's see — where am I?" after losing her place. (I've waited all my life to hear a lector say that!)

Then Annie flipped to a piece of ripped coloring book which served as a page marker and read about Moses and The Ten Commandments . . . which she initially called the Ten Commitments. Actually, she read only seven commandments because she forgot to turn the page to pick up the last three. Jeff played piano while he and Annie sang "Go Down, Moses."

Next, Jeff (an action kind of kid) read about the Israelites and the Wall of Jericho, followed by a rousing "Joshua Fought the Battle of Jericho."

His second reading, certainly appropriate for a boy who likes being one of the guys, was about the selection of the Twelve Disciples. This inspired Annie to sing an impromptu song about the Apostles, which she enhanced with an interpretive dance.

To close, the kids asked us to join hands for a prayer.

As we started to form a circle, I glanced at Lyle. He was wearing a well-worn bathrobe and a pair of old glasses held together with a safety pin. Most Sundays he wears his very best to church and then dons a choir robe for the 10:30 service. When he walks down the aisle with the choir — with his bald head all shiny clean and his half-glasses perched on the end of his nose and his choir robe flapping — he looks like the wisest, kindest angel ever! He's the right man for me, I thought — all spruced up or in an old bathrobe, he's right for me.

I looked at the kids, kids I'd had pretty late in life. They had created a wonderful worship service! They'd planned it together (with no teasing or bossing) and shared in its execution. They're talented, I thought. I hear Annie read nearly every night, but this morning's readings made me aware that she's a remarkable reader. And Jeff's piano — even with little time to practice their selections — sounded really great. He's becoming a fine musician, I realized.

As we joined hands, I bowed my head . . . to see my giant pink piggy slippers staring up at me as I began to pray.

Just minutes later, we were all in the kitchen. I started some pancake batter while Lyle got out the bacon, and Jeff and Annie set the table.

I stopped and looked at this wonderful group of souls I was traveling through life with. How miraculous that we are all together! How blessed my life has been! Can heaven be sweeter than this, I wondered?!!

And the grace of God was everywhere I looked.

July 1992

Make a Joyful Noise

Three Christmases ago, an evening of holiday shopping which started out as great fun was quickly transformed into a family headache.

While my older kids enjoyed the mall, I stayed with three-year-old Annie as she talked with Santa. That done, we all headed out to meet Dad for dinner at a nearby restaurant.

As we passed a shoe store, Annie said, "I want a pair of red shoes, Mommy."

"Your black shoes still fit fine, Sweetheart," I said.

"Well," snapped Annie, still close enough to the terrible two's to remember how the game was played, "*now* I want RED SHOES!!!"

In record time, Annie was crying inconsolably. Then, halfway between the giant rotating Christmas tree and the choir of carolers, Annie got down on the floor and assumed the tantrum position: flat on her stomach, face down, fists clenched at her sides, toes firmly pointed, and her entire body as stiff as a board. She wailed so loudly the carolers stopped singing. A group of shoppers began to form a circle around her.

"I'll never be able to show my face in this mall again, Mother," lamented Lainie.

"Mom, do something! Spank her or something!" begged Eddie.

"Why don't you just buy her the red shoes?" asked eight-year-old Jeff. Then, close to tears himself, he added, "I'll give you the money!"

I picked up Annie under my arm and carried her to the car as if she were a three-foot-long plank. For what seemed an eternity, we drove in a sea of screaming, until at last Annie was spent. Silence prevailed.

I was exhausted. And sorry for myself. This was supposed to have been such a great time. Instead Annie had had a public temper tantrum, we were all humiliated, and I was late for my husband. What an evening.

Jeff broke the silence. "Annie, what did you and Santa talk about?"

Annie answered weakly, "I don't remember."

Eddie turned to Lainie. "I think Annie has amnesia," he deadpanned.

Lainie nodded. "A textbook case: amnesia brought on by a conniption fit."

I couldn't help but giggle. Then Lainie and Eddie laughed. Then Jeff. And finally Annie joined in the laughter. We laughed a long, long, time.

At that moment, I realized how happy I was. I had terrific kids — these four with me and two more at college. They were vibrant. They were free. They were healthy. They were spontaneous. We could afford to go out to dinner. We liked spending time together. We had a car. Annie had black shoes . . . with dreams of red shoes! Lyle was waiting for me. Life was great!

Sometimes joy is revealed through a shout and sometimes through a whisper. But always joy itself is present in God's world. We simply must learn to hear it.

It's Christmas. Shhh. Listen for the joy.

November 1991

Queen for a Lifetime

A few years ago, Lyle and I took the kids to a neighborhood concert. While our pre-schooler Annie was getting herself seated, she bumped half a dozen folding chairs in our row. An older man sitting behind us shot her a nasty look. He "hrumphed" and abruptly shoved them back in place. Then he crossed his arms, frowned, and settled in for the music.

Annie kneeled backwards in her chair, studying the gentleman. After several minutes of this scrutiny, she spoke to him.

They were both wearing red, she noted. Her name was Annie; what was his, she asked. She likes Shari Lewis music; what kind did he like, she wondered. Reluctantly at first, the man answered her. Then he began actually conversing with her. He relaxed. He became animated. He even giggled once! After just a few minutes, he actually looked ten years younger! And Annie was beaming because she had made him happy.

"Annie," he said as the lights flashed, indicating the concert was about to begin, "you have a great smile."

"Thank you," Annie replied politely. She continued innocently, smoothing her skirt, "I also have a great body. And when I grow up," she stated matter-of-factly, "my man will say, 'I am so happy to know a woman like you who has such a great body.'" Just then the lights dimmed and the music began.

I guess I'm responsible for this outrageous attitude of Annie's. (I'll take no responsibility for her "my man" phraseology, however. We discussed that at length later, I can assure you.) You see, it took me almost fifty years to accept my body. But I wanted Annie to grow up having a positive image of all aspects of herself, including her body. It's well-cared for, functional, and in short, beautiful! So from the time she was a baby, every time I bathed Annie — when I scrubbed her little toes or shampooed her hair or dried her with a big, fluffy towel — I told her what a wonderful little body she had. I guess when the old gentleman commented on her great smile, she felt obligated to inform him that she had other terrific parts as well.

After her ballet class a few days later, Annie stood in front of the mirror in my bedroom. "When I hold my arms and shoulders the way Miss Diane showed me," she said, studying herself in wonder, "I look just like a queen."

"You are a queen, Annie," I said. She turned to me, looking mildly surprised. "And so am I. And so is everyone — a queen or king. But some people don't realize it until their lives are half over. Others never know. You're one the of lucky ones: You've discovered it while you're still very young."

She mulled this over; then she smiled from deep inside herself. "I love you, Mommy," she bubbled, moving away from the mirror and into my lap. "I love my whole family," she sighed. Then very softly, haltingly, she added, "I love myself, too, Mom. Is that okay?"

"It's good, Annie," I said as I rocked her. "Loving yourself frees you to love others. That's probably our most important job, loving others. Certainly it's one of a queen's most important jobs."

We rocked for a while. Then, without another word, Annie kissed me, hopped down, and moved on to some new life-adventure.

But I sat there, imagining what life would be like if all the children grew up believing in themselves. I pictured a world of people who were creative, joyful, and kind. People so at home with themselves they gave and accepted love with ease . . . because they had been allowed to freely love all God's children — including themselves.

I sat and rocked and imagined what it could be like . . . and

wondered if the old gentleman at the concert would ever be
the same.

October 1993

Random Thoughts

Facing the Painful Truth
At a football game at Jeff's high school, the running back
jammed his finger going for a catch. He hopped around,
holding his sore hand, grimacing. The quarterback ran to
him, and, as they talked, comforted his teammate by
rubbing his shoulders. It was so sweet! In no time at all,
the running back was fine and in the game once again.

What a change from when I was in high school! Then an
injured athlete would sooner die than cry! If that tough-no-
matter-what attitude is leaving the sports arena, I'm glad.

I've learned I heal faster when I face my pain, give my
family and friends a chance to show their concern toward
me, and graciously accept their loving compassion.

Doesn't this work the same for jocks, too? For young and
old? Female and male? Physical pain and emotional pain?

*A major triumph for Annie was learning how
to use the water dispenser in our refrigerator.
Once victorious, she didn't want to stop!*

Press On

My son Jeff needed a dress shirt for his first junior high dance. We had *clean* but we didn't have *ironed*. I thought, "Jeff won't like this, but it's time he learned how to iron."

Standing in front of the ironing board in the basement, wearing just his trousers and socks, Jeff gave me his full attention — which was the first clue that this lesson had more to it than met the eye — as I talked him through the steps. He flashed me one of his all-time great smiles as he picked up the iron. "What is going on here?" I wondered as he began.

After Jeff ironed the back yoke, he made two fists high in the air and hooted, "YES!" When he finished the cuffs and sleeves, he spun himself around on one foot and did a Three Stooges hand jive before picking up the iron again. When he pressed the collar and put the finishing touches on the shirt, he swung his hips from side to side several times and poked imaginary holes into the air with both his index fingers. Then he grabbed the pressed shirt, held it over his head, and ran around the basement singing the theme from "Rocky."

I couldn't help but think, "If he reacts like this to ironing, maybe this would be a good time to teach him how to disinfect the garbage cans and polish the silver."

As Jeff took one last victory lap around the pool table, I figured out what was really happening: Learning how to iron took Jeff one step closer to self-sufficiency. He was proud as well as jubilant . . . and profoundly impressed with himself.

Learning — of almost any variety — makes us feel powerful. I still remember the heady feeling I had years ago when I learned cursive writing. When my son Eddie mastered tying his shoes, he reacted with same elation adults have when they land that big contract or bake a perfect soufflé. My husband Lyle says he actually felt taller the first time he walked to town all by himself at age ten.

In minutes, Jeff went from non-ironer to one-who-tends-his-own-clothes. And there at the ironing board, I celebrated this life passage with my son. A most unusual "transition of significance," isn't it, but that's what it was to Jeff. He was growing up.

When life is good and gentle, we grow up in small steps, not in leaps. We are eased, one small step after another, into adulthood. With time to savor the victory of each stride. To revel in the triumph of it. To feel the weight of our own power as we move through life, surer and surer as we go.

The small victory is a thing of wonder, even for adults. There is one for you in your life right now. Recognize it. Celebrate it. And then — in joy — press on.

October 1994

Random Thoughts

Among the Clouds
As I began a trip involving stopovers in several cities, the stewardess examined my ticket and asked me, "What is your final destination?"

I knew the answer right off. "Heaven, I hope."

Index

About the Author

Marie Clapper and her husband Lyle have six children . . . two are his, two are hers, and two are theirs. She spends her time with her family; the business she and Lyle own and operate; and friendships formed at work, at church, and throughout her life.

Marie is president/publisher of Clapper Communications Companies, publishers of *Crafts 'n Things, Pack-O-Fun, Painting, The Cross Stitcher,* and *Bridal Crafts.* She joined the 43-year-old Des Plaines, Illinois, company in 1976 as a writer for *Pack-O-Fun.*

Clapper, who has been listed in Who's Who since 1988, is on the Boards of Directors of the Magazine Publishers of America and the Hobby Industry Association.

Photo: Jennifer Girrard (Chicago)

In addition to writing *EveryDay Matters*, Marie Clapper is president of Clapper Communications Companies, which has published craft magazines since 1951. Titles include: *Crafts 'n Things*, *Pack-O-Fun*, *Painting*, *The Cross Stitcher*, and *Bridal Crafts*. All these titles are sold in food, drug, and craft stores around the country.

Subscription Information

Crafts 'n Things carries a wide variety of complete how-to's for craft projects. It is the top-selling craft publication on the newsstand. In each issue, you'll find over 40 projects, ideas, how-to's and tips for beginner to advanced crafters. Our exclusive single-sided, full-size patterns mean you never have to trace a pattern! Subscription: $14.97 + $2 postage. 1 year/10 issues.

Pack-O-Fun features a variety of crafts, games, and stories for families, groups, organizations and schools. Perfect for families and teachers with kids ages 6-12. Subscription: $14.97. 1 year/6 issues.

Painting magazine includes skills, techniques and patterns for beginner to advanced painters — from weekend dabblers to decorative artists. In each issue, original designs are offered for a variety of surfaces, subjects, and media. Full-size patterns, step-by-step instructions, and large color photographs make painting easy. Subscription: $19.95 + $2 postage. 1 year/6 issues.

The Cross Stitcher magazine is the premier cross stitch magazine, averaging over 25 original cross-stitch patterns per issue. Florals, wildlife, humor, holiday, and inspirational designs in every issue. Subscription: $14.97 + $2 postage. 1 year/6 issue.

If you would like a free trial issue of any of the above magazines, please call or write the Clapper office. You'll receive a trial issue promptly. Later an invoice for a 1 year subscription will be mailed to you. If you like the trial issue, please pay the invoice. If you don't like the trial issue, simply write "cancel" on the invoice. You will be under no further obligation.

Clapper Communications Companies
2400 Devon, Suite 375
Dept. 40096
Des Plaines, IL 60018-4618
1-800-444-0441

Would you like additional copies of *EveryDay Matters*?

If you would like additional copies of *EveryDay Matters*, please visit your local bookstore.

Or send $12.95 (plus $1.95 shipping and handling) for each book (Illinois deliveries must add 7% sales tax) to:

Pack-O-Fun, Inc.
Dept. REO996
2400 Devon Avenue, Suite 375
Des Plaines, IL 60018-4618

Or call 1-800-272-3871.